A Student's Guide to the
internet

A Student's Guide to the

internet

EXPLORING
THE WORLD WIDE WEB,
GOPHERSPACE,
ELECTRONIC MAIL,
AND MORE!

by Elizabeth L. Marshall

The Millbrook Press
Brookfield, Connecticut

For Jeff, Abigail, and Amanda

Library of Congress Cataloging–in–Publication Data

Marshall, Elizabeth L.
A student's guide to the Internet: exploring the World Wide Web,
Gopherspace, electronic mail, and more! / by Elizabeth L. Marshall.
p.   cm.
Includes bibliographical references and index.
ISBN 1-56294-923-3 (lib. bdg.)
1. Internet (Computer network) 2. Computer network resources. I. Title.
TK5105.875.I57M3675   1996
004.6'7—dc20   96-5163   CIP

Published by The Millbrook Press, Inc.
2 Old New Milford Road, Brookfield, Connecticut 06804
Copyright © 1996 by Elizabeth L. Marshall
Printed in the United States of America
All rights reserved
1 3 5 4 2

Contents

Acknowledgments

This book was written with the help of many people. I wish to thank Mark Pitcavage for introducing me to the World Wide Web and answering my many questions with patience and good humor; Rachel McMichael for reading the manuscript with a teen's eye; and Tobin Anthony, Hans Tallis, and Laura Pate Cunningham for early encouragement and suggestions.

I also wish to thank the teachers and students who shared their enthusiasm for the Internet with me: Nancy Barkhouse at Atlantic View Elementary School; Elisabeth Beubien at the University of Alberta; Kevin G. Carver at West Kings District High School; George Cassuta at North Hagerstown High School; Chris K. Davis, Jerry Fors, and Laura Snider at the Glendale Unified School District; Nancy Ellsworth at the Model Secondary School for the Deaf at Gallaudet University; John Finch at Henderson School; Josh Huang, Twin Cities Free-Net Volunteer; Tom Keeler at Project City Elementary School; Ken Lewandowski, Kerene Tayloe, and Silas Hoxie at Evanston Township High School; Derick Mather at St. Vital School Division; Michael Ochs, k12.ed.science moderator; Pam Miller at Pine-

< 7 >

lands High School; Brian Pugh and Tong Chieng at Westview Centennial Secondary School; the students of Ralph Bunche School; Carlos A. Rivera, "Darkman," and "McMackin" from k12.chat.senior; Susan Wingate at The Lovett School; and Vicki Wright at Crossroads Park and Fairmeadows Elementary Schools.

Finally, special thanks to the participants in Doug Walker's SchoolNet mailing list. Listening to your discussions was most helpful.

< 8 >

A Student's Guide to the

internet

INTRODUCTION

Imagine sitting down in front of a computer and reading notes from your cousin in Chicago and your friend in Australia. After replying to them, you read several dozen messages from people swapping information about your favorite rock group and the upcoming Lollapalooza tour. Once you have added a few comments of your own to the discussion, you decide you had better work on your science paper about lunar exploration.

Still without ever leaving your chair, you begin examining pictures of the moon's surface that you have called up to your computer screen. You have a question about lunar exploration, so you send a message to a scientist who has volunteered to answer student questions. With a computer connection to the Internet, you can accomplish all of this and much more.

< 11 >

So what, exactly, *is* the Internet? And how does it let you do all these things? The Internet links together many computers to create a single enormous computer network that blankets the globe. You can think of it as a worldwide communications system that allows millions of computers to exchange information. That information includes computer programs, written messages, pictures, sound, and even video. With the Internet, you can communicate with anyone else who has a computer with access to the Internet.

WHAT IS A NETWORK? A network is a group of two or more connected computers. Connected means that the computers can exchange files, messages, and other information. The Internet is often described as a "network of networks" because it links together over 6,000 smaller computer networks.

This immense cluster of computers and connections is populated by people, of course. Describing the Internet without mentioning people is like describing a city as just a bunch of tall buildings. Over 45 million people communicate through the Internet. Together they create a place often referred to as "cyberspace." Cyberspace has its own culture and its own version of good manners. Some people think that cyberspace is a community just like a regular neighborhood or town. Other people are very skeptical of this idea. They think that corresponding with computers actually destroys community.

HOW THE INTERNET BEGAN

Who runs this vast city of 45 million inhabitants? Who planned the Internet? Who maintains it? Who controls it? The answer is hard to believe: Nobody. Nobody is in

< 12 >

charge. Cities have their mayors, nations have their kings and queens and presidents and prime ministers, but nobody rules the Internet. It began in the United States but it doesn't belong to the United States. It doesn't belong to anybody. (Or, to flip that idea around, it belongs to everybody, including you.)

Understanding the history of the Internet helps explain why no one is responsible for it. Imagine, for an instant, the world in the late 1960s: no telephone answering machines, no cellular phones, no cable television, no fax machines, no CD players, no videos and VCRs. Certainly no Internet. Only a few computers existed at all, at a few universities and national laboratories. They had been built with money from the United States Department of Defense to perform government work.

The government wondered if there was a way to connect several computers and transmit information between them. This connection would allow researchers who were based in different places to exchange data. The Department of Defense also wanted to create a computer communications system that could continue working even if part of it were destroyed. This meant building a system without a central authority. It also meant building a system that allowed data traveling from one computer to another to select the best route from a number of possible routes. If one route was destroyed, the information could still arrive by traveling along another route. If the United States were ever attacked, even with a nuclear strike, communication and computer-based research could still continue. In 1969, computers at the University of California, Los Angeles; the Stanford Research Institute; the University of California, Santa Barbara; and the University of Utah were successfully connected. The Internet was born.

More and more computers were added to this network. At first, it was easy to keep track of them. They were at universities or government laboratories. The connections between these computers formed the backbone

< 13 >

of the quickly expanding Internet. Pretty soon, as computer technology spread, other local computer networks were built. Some were at corporations; most were still at universities and government agencies. Each institution bought its own computers and maintained its own computer system. If it connected its local network to the Internet, then the institution took part in the expense and effort of maintaining the Internet. Running the Internet eventually became a shared responsibility rather than the burden of a single organization such as the federal government.

For many years, scientists and computer experts who worked on university campuses or at government agencies were the primary users of the Internet. With the Internet, they sent data to their colleagues and discussed the technical aspects of their fields. But they also swapped messages, told jokes, and debated politics and other nontechnical issues. Clearly the Internet could be used for more than computer work. By the late 1980s, many college campuses established computer labs and gave Internet access to every student. Once considered the province of computer scientists and other eggheads, the Internet was rapidly losing its reputation as a tool for nerds.

WHAT IS A FREE-NET? Is it the same as the Internet? A Free-Net is a community-based network that links local electronic resources, from the library card catalog to calendars of community events to government information. A connection to a Free-Net is free and made by using the telephone line to dial into the system. (To do this, you will need a personal computer and a device known as a modem that connects the computer to the phone system.) Many Free-Nets are connected to the Internet.

< 14 >

In the meantime, commercial online services like CompuServe, GEnie, and Prodigy were growing in popularity. When a new online service, America Online, debuted in 1991, it quickly signed up hundreds of thousands of subscribers. These services made it easy for regular people, without Internet access, to communicate with others who shared their interests—no matter how far away they lived. Although modeled on the Internet, commercial online services were separate from it. Each one formed its own exclusive network.

America Online is not the same as the Internet. And neither is CompuServe, Prodigy, Delphi Internet, GEnie, Microsoft Network, or any one of the other commercial online services. Each of these services has a central headquarters and is carefully regulated. They offer their subscribers many unique features, like exclusive live interviews with celebrities, online encyclopedias and newspapers, forums for discussion, and live "chat" rooms. If you do not subscribe to the service for a monthly fee, you cannot access its features. Even if you have Internet access, you still cannot use features on Prodigy or America Online.

Each commercial service forms its own community of subscribers. Compared to the 45 million Internet users, these communities are very small. The largest commercial services have only three or four million subscribers.

WHAT IS A BULLETIN BOARD SERVICE (BBS)? A BBS is typically operated by an individual or organization and is focused on a particular hobby or interest. It operates like a miniature version of commercial online services and a subscription fee is usually charged. A connection to a BBS is made with a personal computer and a modem connected to the user's telephone system. Some BBSs are connected to the Internet but most are not.

< 15 >

Many subscribers to the commercial services, however, can now gain access via these services to the unregulated world of the Internet.

By 1994, interest in the Internet exploded. Some people discovered they had access to the Internet through their universities or jobs. But many others, who weren't lucky enough to have free Internet access, wanted to become citizens of cyberspace. And they were willing to pay for the opportunity. The commercial online services scrambled to offer their subscribers a gateway to the Internet. At the same time, companies that provided direct access to the Internet for a monthly fee, known as Internet service providers, sprang up across the United States.

Today, more and more schools are providing their students with access to the Internet, also known as the Net. This book is your introduction to cyberspace and its citizens. For the most part, it won't tell you the specific commands you might wish to use while exploring the Internet. Each computer system is slightly different. A discussion of all the different types of systems you might encounter on your school's computers would require a book much longer than this one. (Such books exist, of course! See the Internet Resources section.)

For some Internet features, this book will tell you the commands most computer systems use. For other features, it will direct you to your teacher or classmates for help with specific commands. *A Student's Guide to the Internet* is meant to get you on the Net and to show you all the things you can do with it.

Chapters Two through Seven describe the features of the Internet that are most frequently used in the classroom by middle and high school students: electronic mail, newsgroups, Gopher, file transfer protocol, and the World Wide Web. Chapter Eight presents a variety of group projects to show you the many different ways you can collaborate with students at other schools over the

< 16 >

Internet. Chapter Nine explains how you can use the Internet as your own personal publisher. Chapter Ten offers tips for using the Internet for research papers and evaluating the information you find online. Chapter Eleven tells you how to play it safe on the Internet. The Resources section at the end provides you with some Internet locations to get you started.

< 17 >

ELECTRONIC MAIL

From your computer, you can send written notes to anyone else who is connected to the Internet. These notes are called "electronic mail." Most people refer to them simply as e-mail.

E-mail has many advantages over letters sent by the U.S. Postal Service. Think of all the steps involved when you send a letter to a friend: First you write the letter. Then you must fold it into an envelope, look up your friend's address, write the address on the envelope, attach a stamp, and drop it in the mailbox. So many steps! If you're sending it within the United States, it will arrive in a few days. If you're mailing it overseas, it could take weeks.

E-mail is much, much easier. You write the message while seated at your computer. When you're done, you type a command and it's sent. Whether your friend

< 19 >

is nearby or a world away, the message should arrive within minutes, hours at most. No wonder computer users call letters sent through the U.S. Postal Service "snail mail!"

In some ways, E-mail is more like a phone call than a letter. e-mail arrives almost that quickly and it also travels electronically. Yet it's more convenient than a phone call since it doesn't need to be answered immediately. It can be read and answered whenever it is most convenient. This feature is especially important for busy people.

WHO CAN I WRITE TO?

But what if you don't know another single person who uses the Internet except your classmates?

Do you think you have to know someone personally before you can write to him or her? Think again. If you hear a group of people talking about something that interests you, you usually join in, whether you know the people or not. This is especially true if you're all gathered at the same event, whether it be a bar mitzvah, a party, a rock concert, or a track meet. You can use e-mail in the same way to add your own written messages to discussions that interest you—even if you don't know the other people taking part in the discussion.

Newspapers and magazines often refer to the Internet as an "information superhighway." That makes it sound like the Internet is a place to learn about things, like a library or an encyclopedia or a textbook. It makes it sound like this information moves very quickly, and maybe goes into your brain very quickly. But the Internet has also been described as an "electronic town square." In this image, the Internet is a place where people gather together and talk, exchange ideas, even have disagreements.

Communication is the Internet's most powerful function. By communicating, people can see things in new

< 20 >

ways. They get the chance to walk in someone else's shoes. They can discover what another person's country or life is like. They can learn what it means to be a scientist or to give birth to triplets or to prepare for the Olympics. They can ask questions about current events in another part of the world and get answers from someone who lives there. They are less dependent on television and newspaper reporters for their news.

With e-mail, you can easily and almost instantly be in touch with many, many people around the world. Some of your correspondence will be one-on-one, from you to one other person. But you can also send messages to hundreds and thousands of people at a time.

You'll also want to use e-mail to contact experts whose knowledge might be useful for a school project you're working on. People who would not want to be bothered by phone calls are often willing to answer e-mail messages sent by students. You can write to the president and vice-president of the United States with e-mail. You can probably also write to your representative in Congress. You can even write to celebrities, authors, and athletes if you know their e-mail address.

Chapter Three will take a look at using newsgroups to join conversations in the electronic town square.

This is what a typical e-mail message looks like:

Message 3/9 From Liz Marshall
Subject: Happy Birthday, Jeff!
To: jseiken@magnus.acs.ohio-state.edu
Date: Thu, 31 Aug 1995 08:57:34 -0400 (EDT)
Dear Jeff,
Happy Birthday! Hope you're having fun...wish we could be there.
Liz, Abby, and Amanda

< 21 >

Each e-mail system, known as a mail program or mailer, is slightly different. Some popular e-mail programs are Berkely mail, elm, xmail, and pine. On your school's system, you may have to type a letter command, like **m**, to send a message. Or you may have to point and click on an icon. Ask your teacher what commands your particular computer mail system uses. Learn how to use the **help** command. To get started with e-mail, you will need to learn the commands for these basic functions:

How to read a message sent to you.

How to reply to a message sent to you.

How to send a message.

How to delete old messages.

How to save messages.

W rite to the president! (Or the vice president or the first lady.) Use these e-mail addresses:

president@whitehouse.gov
vice.president@whitehouse.gov
first.lady@whitehouse.gov

DECODING E-MAIL ADDRESSES

E-mail addresses are always written as a long string of letters and symbols. There are no spaces in e-mail addresses. Although a person's e-mail address may look very confusing at first, you can often decode it and learn something about the person with whom you are communicating.

Here's an example. When I was a student at the University of Pittsburgh, my e-mail address looked like this:

< 22 >

elmst2@unix.cis.pitt.edu

The @ symbol stands for "at." This address would be read as "elmst2 at unix.cis.pitt.edu." The first three letters correspond to my full name, Elizabeth L. Marshall. The "st2" indicates that I was a student and that I was the second student with the initials ELM. The letters "edu" at the end of an address stand for "educational." My access to the Internet was through an educational institution.

The rest of the address is less easy to decipher. "Unix" is the name of a computer operating system. "Pitt" stands for the University of Pittsburgh. And "cis" stands for Computer Information Services, an office within the university.

Every e-mail address is made up of three parts: the person's name, the @ symbol, and the domain. (You can think of the domain as the electronic address of the person's institution.) The person's name is very often not their usual name, but rather the name they use to log onto their computer, like "elmst2." This is called their login name.

The domain part of an e-mail address contains an easily identifiable suffix. For every country of the world, a suffix exists that shows which nation the message was sent from. Some examples are:

ca	Canada
de	Germany
uk	United Kingdom
ch	Switzerland
au	Australia
it	Italy

Sometimes the address also includes an abbreviation for a state or province or city as well. Here are two examples

< 23 >

of e-mail suffixes that contain an abbreviation for a particular city:

north-york.on.ca	North York, Ontario, Canada
co.oh.us	Columbus, Ohio, USA

Many e-mail addresses, especially in the United States, don't follow this format, however. Instead, the final suffix describes, in a general way, the kind of place from which the message was sent.

edu	educational
com	commercial
gov	government
org	organization
mil	military
net	network

The rest of the information in the domain is related to the computer user's network system. Sometimes e-mail addresses are easy to figure out. Try this one:

joannashmo@freenet.co.oh.us

Did you guess that it was Joanna Shmo in Columbus, Ohio, USA, using a network called freenet? The next one is harder. Only parts of it are easily understood:

joeshmo@rs710.gsfc.nasa.gov

"Government" is obvious. So is "NASA," the space agency. Joe Shmo must work for NASA. The rest of the address is more difficult. "GSFC" stands for Goddard Space Flight Center and the symbols "rs710" are needed to route the message correctly.

As a general rule of thumb, people who use the Internet through their school or job have e-mail addresses that contain a version of their real names. People who use the Internet through a commercial service, however, often

< 24 >

have e-mail addresses that *don't* contain their real names. They may have a number or a screen name instead. The screen name is a nickname the person adopts and often refers to a hobby or other interest. Three of the major commercial services, America Online, CompuServe, and Prodigy, use distinctive e-mail address domains that you can quickly learn to recognize when you see them on the Internet.

▶ **TIP** E-mail addresses can be written in either uppercase (ELMST2@UNIX.CIS.PITT.EDU) or lowercase (elmst2@unix.cis.pitt.edu). In other words, they are not case-sensitive. Yet Internet custom is to write e-mail addresses in lowercase.

CompuServe's login name is a series of numbers divided by a period and followed by "@compuserve.com." For example:

71111.1111@compuserve.com

The America Online login name is a nickname followed by "@aol.com." Example:

Babyface@aol.com

The Prodigy login name is a nickname followed by "@prodigy.com." Example:

Babyface@prodigy.com

CHAIN LETTERS ON THE INTERNET Electronic chain letters, like ordinary chain letters, depend on people responding to them and then passing them along so that others can read them and respond. Although they may sound harmless, they are often

< 25 >

annoying, sometimes illegal, frequently out-of-date, and always a waste of network resources. They take up valuable electronic storage space and can clog high-speed networks.

"Make Money Fast" is a frequently seen message on the Net. Ignore it! This kind of promise usually disguises a pyramid scheme. In a pyramid scheme, only the people at the beginning of the scheme (the "top" of the pyramid) stand a chance of making money. For this reason, some states ban pyramid schemes.

You might also get a request to send get-well cards to a dying boy. This is a very outdated message. The boy, Craig Shergold of Surrey, England, received 33 million get-well cards several years ago while he was undergoing chemotherapy for cancer. After he won the Guiness Book of World Records title for "most greeting cards received," the book closed that category. In March 1991, Craig underwent a successful operation to remove a brain tumor.

E-mail addresses are often long and complicated. That doesn't mean you have to type out a complicated e-mail address every time you write a friend, however. Most mail programs offer you a way to substitute an easy-to-remember word for your friend's e-mail address. If you wrote to me frequently, you could use a function of your mail program to substitute the word **liz** for my e-mail address. A word substituted for an e-mail address is known as an alias.

Remember, you can get started reading and sending e-mail with just a few basic commands: read, send, reply, delete, and save mail. Learning how to use aliases is useful, too. Mail programs are typically very simple.

< 26 >

Usually you just need to make a selection from a menu of choices or use a one-letter command (like **r** for reply). Choose the **help** command or ask your teacher to help you learn more options.

< 27 >

NEWSGROUPS AND MAILING LISTS

On the Internet, you can communicate with many, many
people at once with just one message. You do this without learning hundreds of e-mail addresses by posting
your message to public discussions on the Internet, ones
that are accessible to every single Internet user. Newsgroups and mailing lists are two types of public forums
on the Internet that allow you to join in written communication with other people who share your interest.

WHAT IS A NEWSGROUP?

A newsgroup is a forum where people post their opinions about a particular topic. They exchange ideas, share
information, provide support, and argue, sometimes
politely and sometimes not. The conversation
builds,message by message, as people read the messages, type their own, read the replies, write some more,

< 29 >

change the subject, read the new replies to the new subject, and so on. Newsgroups are a place to go for entertainment and information, gossip and humor, thoughtful testimony, and wild speculation.

B e sure to use proper jargon! The messages that appear in newsgroups are called "articles." People don't send or mail articles to a newsgroup; they "post" them. A "thread" is a series of articles all related to the same subject.

Some newsgroups are moderated newsgroups. The articles posted to a moderated newsgroup have been reviewed and and approved by a person (or group of people). The identity of this moderator is known to the subscribers of the newsgroup. The moderator works to make sure that articles sent to the newsgroup are on-topic and relevant. Unless a newsgroup is described as moderated, you can assume that it is not moderated. Most newsgroups are not moderated.

Over fourteen thousand newsgroups exist, on almost every subject imaginable. Here is a very tiny sample of available newsgroups:

Newsgroup name	_Subject_
alt.activism	Political activism
alt.astrology	Astrology
alt.college.fraternities	College fraternities
alt.fan.douglas-adams	Books by Douglas Adams
alt.folklore.ghost-stories	Ghost stories
alt.tv.simpsons	The Simpsons TV show
alt.desert-storm.facts	Persian Gulf War
alt.rap	Rap music
alt.support.stop-smoking	Kick the habit
rec.arts.movies.people	Movie stars

< 30 >

rec.arts.movies.current-films	Current films
rec.arts.movies.past-films	Old movies
rec.arts.comics.marketplace	Buy and sell comics
rec.arts.tv.soaps.abc	Soap operas on ABC
rec.food.cooking	Cooking
rec.pets.birds	Parakeets and other birds
rec.sport.football.pro	Pro football
soc.culture.celtic	Celtic culture
soc.culture.brazil	Brazilian culture
comp.os.ms-windows.misc	Microsoft Windows
comp.sys.amiga.games	Amiga games
misc.kids.computer	Kids using computers
misc.taxes	Tax laws
sci.astro	Astronomy
sci.agriculture	Agriculture and farming
talk.politics.animals	Debate over animal use
talk.politics.guns	Debate over gun ownership

Some groups are relatively small and discussion moves slowly. Other groups are very active, receiving hundreds of new articles a day!

Newsgroup names always start with a prefix. This prefix gives you an immediate sense of what the group is about.

comp	computers
news	newsgroup and Internet news
rec	recreation
sci	sciences
soc	social interests
talk	debates
misc	miscellaneous
alt	"alternate" topics that don't fit under any other prefix

Newsgroups occasionally begin with a regional prefix, like **dc** for Washington, D.C. or **osu** for Ohio State University or **az** for Arizona.

< 31 >

Newsgroups are also known as network news. The system that distributes them is called USENET. There are also private newsgroups, available for a fee, like the seventy-six moderated newsgroups maintained by the Global SchoolNet Foundation.

It is in the newsgroups that the Internet seems most like an electronic town square. In a town square, people talk face to face. That doesn't happen in the newsgroups, of course. Words must substitute for voices. And it may take several days for one article to reply to another. But in a newsgroup, people often describe their own personal experiences with a great deal of sincerity and emotion. They are eager to share the wisdom they've gained through their own trial and error. These are true stories, coming to you direct from the source.

Newsgroups can give you a perspective on current events that may be very different than what you find on TV or in the newspaper. The event doesn't have to be as monumental as a bombing or an earthquake, either. Newsgroup contributors also write about watching an Olympic event or shaking hands with a presidential candidate. Descriptions of very ordinary events, like bringing home a new puppy or breaking up with a boyfriend, can also be found in newsgroups.

Many newsgroups have a scholarly or professional theme, like the Civil War or astronomy. Others are fan clubs, created around popular bands or television shows or actors. Some groups offer information about a disease, like arthritis or AIDS, while also offering tips and support for people with the disease.

NEWSGROUPS FOR KIDS AND TEENS

A few dozen newsgroups are devoted specifically to children, teens, and teachers. They begin with the prefix **k12**. Three of these newsgroups, divided according to the age of students, exist simply for open discussion. These newsgroups are:

< 32 >

k12.chat.elementary	discussion for elementary students
k12.chat.junior	discussion for junior high students
k12.chat.senior	discussion for senior high students

A dozen or so are organized according to school subjects. These are primarily for teachers of those subjects, but student articles are welcome, too. In k12.ed.science, for instance, students often post questions related to science projects they are working on. Scientists, professors, and other experts reply to their questions with encouragement and advice. Students also take part in ongoing discussions related to various issues in science. Here are the newsgroups devoted to specific school subjects:

k12.ed.art	art
k12.ed.business	business
k12.ed.comp.literacy	computer literacy
k12.ed.health-pe	health and physical education
k12.ed.life-skills	home economics and career education
k12.ed.math	math
k12.ed.music	music
k12.ed.science	science
k12.ed.soc-studies	social studies
k12.ed.special	special education
k12.ed.tag	talented and gifted

Four newsgroups devoted to the study of foreign languages allow students to practice French, Spanish, German, and Russian. Here are their names:

k12.lang.deutsch-eng	German-English
k12.lang.esp-eng	Spanish-English
k12.lang.francais	French-English
k12.lang.russian	Russian-English

In an effort to protect its students from the unregulated, unmediated, and unchaperoned world of the Internet, your school might elect to subscribe only to the k12

< 33 >

newsgroups. Be forewarned, however. On occasion, even these groups, particularly the discussion groups, contain language and topics that some people find controversial and objectionable.

⚠️ **WARNING** Don't ever post personal information about yourself, such as your phone number or home address, in a public place on the Internet like a newsgroup.

If someone in the newsgroup acts in a suspicious manner, tell your teacher and parents. Do not arrange meetings with anyone you meet through a newsgroup. (See Chapter Eleven: Playing It Safe on the Internet.)

CONVERSATIONS IN CYBERSPACE

Here's a sample exchange of articles.

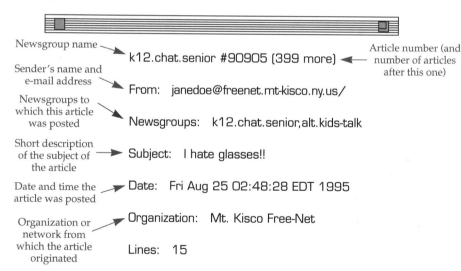

Newsgroup name ➝ k12.chat.senior #90905 (399 more) ⬅ Article number (and number of articles after this one)

Sender's name and e-mail address ➝ From: janedoe@freenet.mt-kisco.ny.us/

Newsgroups to which this article was posted ➝ Newsgroups: k12.chat.senior,alt.kids-talk

Short description of the subject of the article ➝ Subject: I hate glasses!!

Date and time the article was posted ➝ Date: Fri Aug 25 02:48:28 EDT 1995

Organization or network from which the article originated ➝ Organization: Mt. Kisco Free-Net

Lines: 15

My life is over! I'm fifteen years old and the eye doctor just told me I need to get glasses, and I'll probably have to wear them all the time. And the problem with my eyes means I won't be able to use contacts, either. Geekhood, here I come!

< 34 >

I admit I can't see too well, and sometimes it's a problem. But this is such a bad time to start wearing glasses. I wanted to try out for the lead in our school play this year—and whoever heard of a leading lady with goggles on her face?! Not to mention the fact that no guy will ever look at me. What's the saying? "Men never make passes at girls who wear glasses!"

I know I shouldn't be so shallow, but facts are facts. I must be the unluckiest person in the world!!!

k12.chat.senior #90913 (42 + 351 more)
From: T_Smith@hal.sys.state-school.edu (Thomas Smith)
Newsgroups: k12.chat.senior,alt.kids-talk
Subject: Re: Glasses
Date: Fri Aug 25 09:58:55 EDT 1995
Organization: State School
Lines: 8

I know just how you feel. A few years ago my eye doctor told me the same thing. And what did I do? I *NEVER* wore my glasses. And not only did I bump into a lot of people and walls and furniture, I permanently damaged my sight by straining my eyes. Now I have to wear special glasses, and I still can't see very well. So, even if you think they will hurt your social life, you should definitely wear them. I'd give anything now to be a "geek with glasses" who can see!

k12.chat.senior #90940 (36 + 351 more)
From: charlie@spidernet.ivy.va.us (Charlie)
Newsgroups: k12.chat.senior,alt.kids-talk
Subject: Re: I hate glasses!!
Date: Fri Aug 25 16:24:11 EDT 1995
Organization: Virginia Technology Network
Lines: 7

Re: Geek with glasses
I don't think you should worry too much about it. I'm a guy who has lots of friends who wear glasses, some of them girls. And to me, they just wouldn't look like "them" without

< 35 >

their glasses. Pretty soon your glasses will be a part of you—and if you're pretty without glasses, you'll be pretty with them, too. :-) ◄— Smiley (read sideways).
See page 42 for more information

k12.chat.senior #90962 (33 + 351 more)
From: AMS262@montemalaga.schoolnet.edu (Andy)
Newsgroups: k12.chat.senior,alt.kids-talk
Subject: Re: I hate glasses!!
Date: Fri Aug 25 22:22:13 EDT 1995
Organization: Pacific Area Schoolnet
Lines: 9

:Pretty soon your glasses will be a part of you—and if you're
:pretty without glasses, you'll be pretty with them, too. :-)

I totally agree. If you're a great person and fun to be with, guys will look at you no matter what, believe me. And you never know, maybe there's some surgery you can have someday to correct your vision. Until then, you should decide to break the "glasses/geek" stereotype once and for all.

JOINING THE CONVERSATION

To read and send articles to newsgroups, you need a news reader program on your computer system. Dozens of different kinds of news readers exist. Some well-known news readers are rn, trn, tin, and Trumpet. You will need to learn the basic commands for your school's particular news reader.

You will also need to find out what newsgroups are available to you. Do you have access to the thousands of newsgroups? Does your school subscribe to SchoolNet? Are you limited to the k12 newsgroups? Ask your teacher.

If a newsgroup is available to you, you can subscribe to it. Think of subscribing to a newsgroup like subscribing to a magazine. Many magazines exist, obviously, but they aren't going to show up in your mailbox unless you subscribe to them. In the same way, newsgroups won't

< 36 >

automatically appear in your news reader program unless you subscribe to them. The main difference between subscribing to a newsgroup and subscribing to a magazine is that subscribing to a newsgroup is free!

Let's suppose your teacher tells you that all the newsgroups carried by Usenet are available to you. (Unlikely, but let's pretend!) You are really into alternative music and a friend has told you about a newsgroup called "alt.music.alternative" that discusses alternative bands. You tell your computer to go to alt.music.alternative. This subscribes you to this newsgroup. From now on, whenever you use your news reader, you will be prompted to read articles in this newsgroup.

When you begin reading the newsgroup, you discover that hundreds of articles are waiting there. You start with the first, which is the oldest article. It's boring, so you delete it. In fact, you find yourself deleting most of the articles. (Every news reader gives you a way to do this easily.) You read only the interesting ones.

Soon you find yourself in the middle of an argument about one of your favorite bands. Some people think the band is selling out. Others think just the opposite. You find yourself nodding your head in agreement to some of the articles. Other articles seem completely stupid. When you return to the newsgroup the next day, you find that a hundred new articles have been added.

After a few days, you post your own comments to the discussion. Then you decide to change the subject. You need some advice. Can anyone tell you when the next Smashing Pumpkins album is due? You post this question to the group. Later that day, you receive an answer.

WHAT YOU NEED TO KNOW: FROM BEGINNER TO EXPERT

Although news readers are loaded with flashy extras, you can get started after learning just a few basic com-

< 37 >

mands. All a beginner really needs to know is how to find a newsgroup and how to read the articles in it. As you become experienced, however, you will want to explore the capabilities of your particular news reader. The best way to do this is to learn how to use the **help** function on your news reader. (In rn and trn, for example, typing **h** at the prompt will display a list of available commands to choose from.)

Beginners who just want to read newsgroup articles need to learn the commands for these functions:

How to subscribe to a newsgroup.

How to start reading articles.

How to page forward to read a long article.

How to redisplay an article already read.

How to delete articles.

How to skip over unread articles.

How to exit the newsgroup.

How to go to the next newsgroup.

How to unsubscribe from a newsgroup.

Intermediate users who want to read and reply to newsgroup articles need to learn the commands for these functions:

How to send an e-mail reply to the author of a newsgroup article. (Your article goes only to the author, not to the newsgroup.)

How to post a follow-up to an article. (Your article goes to the newsgroup.)

How to post an article to the newsgroup introducing a new subject.

< 38 >

Experts who want more control over what they are reading need to learn the commands for these functions:

How to display the subject line of all articles.

How to select a subject thread.

How to find an article on a particular subject.

How to save an article.

With some news readers, such as Trumpet, it is very easy to perform these functions. All you need to do is point and click your mouse. Other news readers require you to use a variety of keyboard commands.

▶ **T I P** If you are using keyboard commands with your news reader, you will need to pay attention to upper- and lowercase letters. With the news reader rn, for example, **n** means go to the next unread article, while **N** means go to the next article.

DISCUSSION GROUPS THROUGH E-MAIL

Mailing lists, another form of discussion in cyberspace, are very similar to newsgroups. There are mailing lists for all kinds of people on all kinds of subjects. (See the Internet Resources section for several mailing lists for kids and teens.) Mailing lists are often managed by an automatic program known as LISTSERV. For this reason, mailing lists are sometimes called "list servers." The difference between newsgroups and mailing lists lies in the way the two features work.

Reading and posting to newsgroups requires a news reader program. Many people who lack this somewhat specialized option still have access to electronic mail. Mailing lists grew out of the desire to use e-mail to share in group discussions.

< 39 >

To join a mailing list, you need only to be able to send and receive e-mail. Joining a mailing list is known as subscribing. To subscribe (and unsubscribe) to a mailing list, you will need to know its request address.

To subscribe to a mailing list, write an e-mail message to the request address. Leave the subject line of your message blank. In the body of your message, type the word **subscribe** followed by the name of the list and your name. Then send your message. That's all you have to do! (To unsubscribe, send an e-mail message with the word **unsubscribe** followed by the name of the list and your name.)

Here's an example. Let's say Billy Marshall wishes to subscribe to My-View, a mailing list dedicated to creative writing. The request for My-View is **listserv@sjuvm.stjohns.edu** . Billy needs to send an e-mail message to that address. His message looks like this:

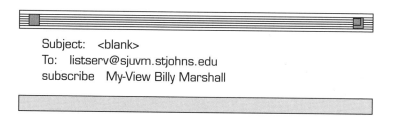

```
Subject:   <blank>
To:   listserv@sjuvm.stjohns.edu
subscribe   My-View Billy Marshall
```

Several minutes after sending an e-mail message to subscribe, you will receive an e-mail message confirming your subscription. Save this message! It often will include useful details about the mailing list, including how to post articles and how to unsubscribe.

Once you've subscribed, the discussion will automatically be sent to you via e-mail. In most respects, it resembles a newsgroup discussion. Some mailing lists arrive once a week. Others come more often. Some lists send a batch of articles in a single, long e-mail article. Other articles in mailing list discussions arrive one at a time. In any event, you will need to keep up with the correspondence

< 40 >

and delete articles after you read them. Otherwise you will quickly become overwhelmed with e-mail.

As with newsgroups, you can add your own comments and questions to a mailing list. Just send an e-mail message to the list address. (This address is different than the subscription or request address.) Your article will then be distributed to everyone on the list.

R EAL-TIME CONVERSATION: INTERNET RELAY CHAT Another communication feature of the Net is Internet Relay Chat. IRC lets you carry on a conversation online. Of course, the conversation is written. (The end result looks something like dialogue for a play.) Furthermore, the people who wish to communicate must all be connected to the Internet at the same time. For more information on the joys of IRC, visit the newsgroup **alt.irc**. To learn how to use it, consult a book that describes IRC in detail. (Or, after reading Chapter Six, obtain a tutorial via anonymous ftp from **cs-ftp.bu.edu** in the directory **/irc/support/** .)

INTERNET + ETIQUETTE = NETIQUETTE

If you're interested in a newsgroup or mailing list subject and can join the conversation with thoughtful comments, go right ahead. That's one of the great things about cyberspace: other people can't discriminate against you simply for being young. In fact, they won't even know you're a teenager unless you tell them.

When you post an article, you're judged simply on the content of your article, not your age, sex, race, or physical condition. For this reason, some people with disabilities have found the Internet an exhilarating place to communicate.

It's great to be judged solely on the content of your articles. But that also makes the writing and organization

< 41 >

of your articles especially important. You can do several things to make sure your articles are both relevant and courteous:

Lurk First

Don't immediately post to a newsgroup that's new to you. Spend some time reading the articles that are posted to it before adding your own ideas. This is known as "lurking" and is highly recommended to avoid duplicating comments and just plain looking stupid.

Read the FAQ

Many newsgroups have prepared statements in response to questions frequently asked by people new to the newsgroup. These statements are known as FAQs (pronounced "facts"), short for Frequently Asked Questions. Read the FAQ of a newsgroup before posting your questions.

How TO FIND FAQS: Each newsgroup regularly posts its own FAQ.

Visit the "answers" newsgroups: alt.answers, rec.answers, comp.answers, misc.answers, and so on. They post the FAQ lists for their particular subject area.

After reading Chapters Five, Six, and Seven, you'll know how to use Gopher, the World Wide Web, and file transfer protocol to find lots of interesting things, including newsgroup FAQs.

Don't Blanket the Internet

If you have something to say, pick one relevant newsgroup to say it to. Posting the same article to two or more groups is known as "cross-posting." Don't do it. If your article seems applicable to many groups, then there's probably something wrong with either your article or your perception of the purpose of newsgroups.

< 42 >

Avoid Flame Wars

Debate is encouraged, even relished, in most news-groups. Don't avoid disagreement, but do avoid insults, name-calling, and other abusive behavior—known as "flames" in cyberspace. Treat people with courtesy. Respond to obvious ignorance with facts and citations. An all-out attack is a "flame war." Comments that are sure to ignite a flame war are known as "flame bait." (Need an example of "flame bait"? It's the thing you say to your little brother to make him go ballistic. It's the phrase that makes your father slam on the car brakes and order you out of the car. In other words, it varies from situation to situation but you'll know it when you hear it.) Flaming will try the patience of those not directly involved. It is a waste of time—and Net resources.

Don't Shout

Using all capital letters is the written equivalent of shouting. ALL CAPITALS MAKE YOU LOOK LIKE YOU'RE THROWING A TEMPER TANTRUM. This is considered very rude. If you need to emphasize something you're saying, use *asterisks* around the word.

Keep It Brief

If you wish to add your comments to a subject, go right ahead. Out of consideration to other people who may have missed the first exchange of articles, include the part of the previous post that is relevant to your response. Don't include all of it—just enough so that others can pick up on the discussion. On the other hand, if your comment consists solely of "I agree" or "Me, too" or "Ditto," resist the urge to post it. Comments like those, completely lacking in content, are also a waste of Net resources.

Use a Dictionary

Communication in cyberspace is solely dependent upon the written word. For this reason, you should check your

< 43 >

spelling and your grammar scrupulously. Basic mistakes in English will distract from your message and erode your credibility. On the other hand, to criticize someone else's spelling and grammar is considered poor manners and, once again, a waste of Net resources. You might also wish to consider that many people on the Internet speak English only as a second (or third or fourth) language.

Two newsgroups are of particular interest to Internet newcomers, or "newbies." Check out: **news. announce.newusers** and **news. newusers.questions** for discussions of netiquette, writing style, and other newsgroup-related topics. (By the way, the term newbie is an insult!)

Here are several computer sites that contain files of FAQs and other newsgroup information. You can read and make copies of these files with file transfer protocol (see Chapter Six).

FTP to rtfm.mit.edu
   select the directory **/pub/rtfm**
FTP to ftp.seas.gwu.edu
   select the directory **/pub/rtfm**
FTP to mirrors.aol.com
   select the directory **/pub/rtfm/usenet**
FTP to ftp.uu.net
   select the directory **/pub/usenet-by-group**

SMILEY FACES AND OTHER CYBERLANGUAGE

When you speak to someone face to face, you listen to their words and read their body language. Even over the phone, the way someone says something can clue you in as to whether they are being sarcastic or sincere, definite or doubtful. In written communication, these subtleties are lost. To make up for them, writers must select their words carefully and readers must be alert to tone, context, and emphasis.

< 44 >

No one wants to work that hard while reading and writing e-mail or newsgroup articles. As a result, an entire alphabet of symbols has been developed to help make the emotional tone of articles very clear. Some of the symbols look like this:

<g>	Grinning
<l>	Laughing
<s> or **<sigh>**	Sighing

Other symbols look like smiley faces. (Look at them sideways!) Smileys are also called "emoticons" (emoticon = emotion + icon).

:-) or **:)**	Just kidding, or I'm smiling
;-) or **;)**	I'm winking
:-(or **:(**	I'm sad

Also frequently seen on the Internet are acronyms used as a kind of emotional shorthand:

BTW	By the way
FYI	For your information
GMAB	Give me a break
HHOK	Ha, ha, only kidding
HHOJ	Ha, ha, only joking
IMO	In my opinion
IMHO	In my humble opinion
LOL	Laughing out loud
RTFM	Read the fine manual. . . if all else fails
YMMV	Your mileage may vary (This information or advice may work slightly differently for you)

Lots and lots of emoticons and acronyms have been invented by clever people, but these are the ones that actually get used. Be warned! Emoticons can be addictive. You might begin to find them creeping into all your correspondence :-) .

< 45 >

GO FOR INFORMATION WITH GOPHER

You have just seen how the Internet lets you communicate with other people through features like e-mail and newsgroups. The Internet is also an information source. One of its most popular information features is known by the odd name of "Gopher." You can think of it as a feature that lets you "go fer" information on the Net.

You can use Gopher to find all kinds of information:

- Academic information on every subject, from archaeology to zoology

- Entire books, from the Bible to *Alice in Wonderland* to *Pride and Prejudice*

- Recipes

- Schedules and locations for live music, theater performances, and sports events

< 47 >

- Cultural information on many states and countries

- Playlists from past Grateful Dead concerts

- Book reviews

- Government information, from census data to White House policy statements to State Department travel warnings to NASA space data

  . . . and much, much more

Many organizations share their knowledge and data with the Internet community through Gopher. When an organization makes information available on the Gopher system, it does so through a Gopher server. The Ralph Bunche School, an elementary school in New York City, has a Gopher server. NASA, the space agency, has a Gopher server. So do many universities and museums. A group of fans have put together a Gopher server about the Grateful Dead. MTV once had a Gopher server, but no longer.

Computer programs that allow people to access Gopher servers are known as Gopher clients. Most people who use Gopher usually don't talk about Gopher servers or Gopher clients, however. They simply say they're going to use Gopher to read their favorite online magazine or to check population figures with the Census Bureau Gopher or to get concert tour updates from the Phish Gopher.

HOW GOPHER GOT ITS NAME Take your pick from these explanations: 1. A gopher digs through the earth, just like the Gopher system digs up information. 2. The word "Gopher" sounds like "go fer," a person whose job it is to run errands and get things. 3. The system was created at the University of Minnesota, where the school mascot is—a Golden Gopher.

< 48 >

Gopher is one of the easiest Internet features to master. You don't need to know a complicated set of commands to use it. Instead, you simply make your request by selecting from a directory of choices.

Although there is not much variation among different kinds of Gopher programs, check with your teacher to see which Gopher program your system uses. The commands described in this chapter are UNIX Gopher commands. Gopher programs that run with Microsoft Windows are similar, but you will point and click with a mouse instead of using keyboard commands.

TELNET

If your computer system lacks a Gopher client, you will have to connect to another computer system to use Gopher. To make your remote connection, you will use a feature known as telnet. In addition to Gopher, telnet can be used to access other Internet features. Although the steps you follow may vary slightly depending upon your computer system, here are the basic commands for using telnet:

1. Before you begin, you will need to know the name of the host system you wish to connect to. Computer books, newsgroup discussions, and mailing lists are all places where you can find names of computer systems that permit telnet access for a variety of purposes, including the use of Gopher.

2. At your computer system's prompt, type **telnet** followed by a space and the host system name. Press **Enter**. (After each of these commands you will need to press Enter.)

EXAMPLE: **telnet cat.ohiolink.edu**

3. You will be asked to type a login name. (For most public Gophers, you will type **gopher** .)

< 49 >

4. You may be asked what kind of terminal you are using. (Most systems use vt 100.)

5. You're ready to go to work!

6. To disconnect, type **logout** or **exit** or whatever the system prompts you to type.

H ere are a few public Gophers that you can telnet to:

uxl.cso.uiuc.edu	Illinois
inform.umd.edu	Maryland
ecosys.drdr.virginia.edu	Virginia
cat.ohiolink.edu	Ohio
gopher.msu.edu	Michigan

If you have access to the World Wide Web (see Chapter Seven) you can use it to connect to Gopher.

WORKING WITH DIRECTORIES

All the information in Gopher is organized in directories, also called menus. Let's say that you wanted to create a Gopher server that describes your home town. You would have to categorize the information in a series of menus.

Here's how your menu might look:

1. Location of my home town

2. People in my home town

3. Buildings in my home town

4. History of my home town

5. Calendar of upcoming events in my home town

< 50 >

People could learn more about your hometown by selecting one of the choices. You might think of the directory as an outline.

Within Gopher, menu items very often lead you to more menus and more choices. Let's look at an actual Gopher server created by students and teachers at the Ralph Bunche School in New York City. The students there are in grades three to six. Here is how they organized information about their school. Their menu has twelve categories:

Ralph Bunche School ("The world's first elementary school")

1. About the Ralph Bunche School
2. Search Titles On The RBS Gopher <?>
3. Recent Ralph Bunche School newspaper stories/
4. Shadows Science Project/
5. Student Work/
6. Junior High School 43/
7. RBS Goes to NECC 94/
8. FCC Chair Reed Hundt Visits RBS/
9. Student Introductions/
10. BBN's National School Network Testbed/
11. Information about GN, a gopher/WWW server/
12. RBS.GIF <Picture>

Notice that some of these items end with a forward slash (/). Others do not. If you choose an item with a forward slash, you will be presented with another menu of choices. If you choose an item without a forward slash, you will be presented with a document. Let's choose 1, "About the Ralph Bunche School." To choose an item, place the cursor on the line and press Enter. Or simply type in the number of the item. This item is not followed

< 51 >

by a forward slash so we can expect a document. And that's exactly what appears:

About the Ralph Bunche School (1k)

The Ralph Bunche School

Hi! My name is Renso Vasquez and I am going to tell you about the Ralph Bunche School. The location of the Ralph Bunche School is 425 West 123rd St. in New York City, New York. This school starts at 3rd grade and ends at the 6th grade.

Here at Ralph Bunche we have a mini-school. This is called the Computer School. At the Computer School we learn how to use computers better (the Computer School includes 4th, 5th, and 6th and has 8 classes).

We are also known to have more computer technology than most of the other elementary schools. We also have audio video. We can use cameras and camcorders. We also have a video kids news team, it is called KWN (Kid Witness News). We also have access to the Internet, meaning that we can communicate with other people inside and outside of the United States. We each have addresses like when we are mailing letters to people. My computer address is below under my name.

What I think is that we can use computers for every-thing. I can write a better essay with a computer. I graduat-ed last semester and I am missing out on a lot of cool stuff. Well, if you were me, you would want to return also.

Renso Vasquez
rensov@ralphbunche.rbs.edu

Now let's return to the top menu of twelve items. Use the command **u** (for up) to return to the top menu. (You don't need to press Enter.)

< 52 >

Ralph Bunche School ("The world's first elementary school")

1. About the Ralph Bunche School
2. Search Titles On The RBS Gopher <?>
3. Recent Ralph Bunche School newspaper stories/
4. Shadows Science Project/
5. Student Work/
6. Junior High School 43/
7. RBS Goes to NECC 94/
8. FCC Chair Reed Hundt Visits RBS/
9. Student Introductions/
10. BBN's National School Network Testbed/
11. Information about GN, a gopher/WWW server/
12. RBS.GIF <Picture>

This time, let's choose 5: "Student Work". This item is followed by a forward slash, so we know we're going to be given another menu to look at. Here's what appears:

Student Work

1. Halloween Drawings/
2. Poems/
3. Authors' Point Of View/
4. "Up In A Tree" Poems/
5. "Now Is The Time" Poems/
6. Spanish Alphabet/

Perhaps you're curious about "'Now Is The Time' Poems". Let's choose option #5 to look at that item. The

< 53 >

item is followed by a forward slash, so we can expect another menu.

"Now Is The Time" Poems

1. Introduction to Poems
2. Index to Poems
3. Now Is My Time (Part One)
4. Timmie Sampson <Picture> ·
5. Shek Bangura <Picture>
6. Terence McBryde <Picture>
7. Christopher Glover <Picture>
8. Now Is My Time (Part Two)
9. Takeya Eley <Picture>
10. Zenobia Collins <Picture>
11. Now Is Your Time (Part Three)
12. Tameyer Bell <Picture>
13. Alina Jordan <Picture>
14. Lamar Spencer <Picture>
15. Now Is Your Time (Part Four)
16. Ashante Blue <Picture>
17. Ashanta Saxton <Picture>

Looking at this menu doesn't tell us much about this project. Let's look at #1: "Introduction to Poems" to learn more about it. Notice that #1: "Introduction to Poems" is not followed by a forward slash. We can expect a document.

Introduction to Poems (Ok)

Our class C.S. 6-213 from the Ralph Bunche Computer School in New York City, read a book called Now Is Your

< 54 >

Time by Walter Dean Myers. The book is about African-American History. When we finished, we wrote these poems and drew these pictures to go with these poems. We hope you like this booklet.

Credits
Editor
Tameyer Bell : tameyerb@ralphbunche.rbs.edu

Ah-ha! Now we know what we're likely to find. By using the **u** command, we can return to the "'Now is the Time' Poems" menu. From this menu we could choose a poem to read.

▶ **T I P** Addresses of resources on the Internet are known as Uniform Resource Locators (URLs). The URL of the Ralph Bunche School gopher server is: **gopher://ralphbunche.rbs.edu:70/1** . In some systems you can use the command **o** to go directly to a Gopher address.

EXPLORING THE GOPHER SYSTEM

On the Internet, thousands of Gophers are linked. You can easily move from menu to menu, across the Gopher servers of many different groups from around the world. As you move swiftly from menu to menu, you won't necessarily know whose menu you are looking at or where the information was dished from. The entire system is known as Gopherspace.

In Gopherspace, connections are seamless. Information is grouped by placing similar items together. Gopherspace is easy and fun to explore.

< 55 >

COMMANDS TO USE WITH UNIX GOPHER PROGRAMS

Up and down arrow keys	Move cursor between menu items
Enter	Selects item where you have placed cursor
<number>	Enter the number of the item you wish to view and then press Enter
u	Up to previous menu
spacebar or **Page Down**	Next page
b	Previous page
o	Open a new Gopher (on some systems)
q	Quit Gopher

Here's how your exploration of Gopherspace might start if you were at Ohio State University. This is the first menu university students see when they use Gopher. (The Gopher at Ohio State University is called Oasis.)

OASIS Main Menu

   1. Finding Information on OASIS/
   2. News and Weather/
   3. People Directories/
   4. Opportunities/
   5. Information Resources/

< 56 >

6. Library & Archive Services/
7. Journals & Newsletters/
8. Electronic Bookshelf/
9. OSU Administration/

This menu is capable of sending you in many different directions. Let's select #1: "Finding Information on Oasis." Here's the menu that follows:

Finding Information on OASIS

1. About the OSU Gopher (OASIS)/
2. Keyword Search - OASIS Menus - Titles/
3. Keyword Search - Worldwide Menus - Titles/
4. Useful Off-Campus Resources/
5. What's New On OASIS?/
6. About Ownership of Information on OASIS
7. Multimedia Tools/

This menu offers an entrance into Gopherspace. Let's select #4: "Useful Off-Campus Resources."

Useful Off-Campus Resources

1. About this Menu
2. BUBL Information Service (Subject Guide), (UK)/
3. Clearinghouse of Subject-Oriented Internet Resource Guides/
4. Descriptions of European Networks/
5. EARN Information Service/
6. Educom/

< 57 >

7. Electronic Dictionaries, Gazetteers, etc./
8. European National Entrypoints/
9. Gopher Jewels & Other Subject Trees/
10. MTV Gopher/
11. RIPE NCC (Information Server for the European IP-Network)/
12. Resources for the Researcher/
13. Scholarly Societies/
14. Subject Specific Information Servers/
15. US Government Gopher Servers (UCIs List)/

Again, another long menu with lots of intriguing items. Let's select #12: "Resources for the Researcher."

Resources for the Researcher

1. About the Researcher Menu
2. UIC Office of the Vice Chancellor for Research/
3. Grants and Opportunities/
4. Veronica: Netwide Gopher Menu Search/
5. Aerospace/
6. Agriculture and Forestry/
7. Anthropology and Culture/
8. Arts/
9. Astronomy and Astrophysics/
10. Biology/
11. Chemistry/
12. Computing and Computer Networks/
13. Economics/
14. Education/
15. Environment and Ecology/
16. Geography/
17. Geology and Geophysics/
18. Government, Political Science and Law/
    Page: 1/2

< 58 >

This is the first page of this two-page directory. We're still being presented with lots of categories, but at least they're divided here into various academic areas.

Let's stop our search here. The top level menus in your Gopher system will most likely not look like these. But with a little exploration, you will be able to select the items that will move you to the menus you want.

▶ **TIP** If your computer system runs its own Gopher client, you can move directly to the Gopher of your choice. Simply type **gopher** at your system's prompt, and then the Gopher address, or use the command **o** at any Gopher menu.

KEEPING YOUR PLACE IN GOPHERSPACE

When you first browse through Gopherspace, you are going to find many menu items that you would like to read later. Fortunately, Gopher offers you an easy way to mark items that you wish to return to later. You need not plow through menu after menu to find them again. With four easy commands, you can save your choices for easy access later.

When you find something in Gopher that you wish to keep, place the cursor on the item you would like to save and press **a**, for add. You can do this for as many categories as you like. This creates a personalized menu that you can see by pressing **v** for view. By using the command **A** in a menu, you can save the entire menu to your list. The command **d** deletes items from your list. Using these commands is known as placing "bookmarks" in Gopherspace.

Let's return to the Ralph Bunche School Gopher for an example. We already sampled some of the material in the school's Gopher server. We have a general sense of the kind of information it contains. Nevertheless, we

< 59 >

skipped over many of the items in the top menu, including #3: "Recent Ralph Bunche School newspaper stories" and #9: "Student Introductions." We also bypassed most of the choices in the "Student Work" menu and in the "'Now Is The Time' Poems" menu.

If we use the a command to select #3: "Recent Ralph Bunche School newspaper stories" from the top menu, #1: "Halloween Drawings" and #6: "Spanish Alphabet" from the "Student Work" menu, and #11: "Now Is Your Time (Part Three)" from the "'Now Is The Time' Poems" menu, this is what our personalized menu will look like:

Bookmarks

1. Recent Ralph Bunche School newspaper stories/
2. Halloween Drawings/
3. Spanish Alphabet/
4. Now Is Your Time (Part Three)/

On future visits to Gopherspace, we could view our personalized menu by using the command v.

Now you know the basics of Gopherspace. In the next chapter, you'll learn how to control your Gopher searches even more.

B ookmark Commands for UNIX Gopher Programs

a	Add item to bookmark list
A	Add menu to your bookmark list
v	View bookmark list
d	Delete item from bookmark list

< 60 >

These commands are case-sensitive. In other words, a lowercase **a** is a very different command than an uppercase **A**.

Note: Depending upon your type of Internet access, your personalized menu might not be saved when you exit the system. Ask your teacher if this will happen.

< 61 >

TAKING COMMAND OF GOPHERSPACE

Gopherspace is a great place to browse. It can give you a very good idea of the kinds of resources available on the Net. But browsing is a hit-or-miss affair. You follow your whims, and trust that they will lead you in useful and interesting directions. Sometimes you're going to want to work with Gopher in a more organized way. You might want to be able to collect Gopher's resources on a specific subject, such as archaeology or the Olympic Games or Democratic politics.

This chapter will tell you how to do a subject search of Gopherspace. With a tool known as Veronica, you can gain control over your use of Gopher.

USING A KEYWORD

At times, you're going to want to know whether a Gopher contains information on a particular topic. In the

< 63 >

Ralph Bunche Elementary School Gopher, for instance, you might want to know what the Gopher can tell you about computers at the school. You would like to find every document in the Gopher related to this topic. Another way of saying this is that you would like to do a subject search with the keyword "computers."

The Ralph Bunche Elementary School Gopher allows you to do a subject search from the second item on the main menu. You can tell because the symbol <?> appears at the end of that item. Not all Gophers have this capability. Here's the main menu again:

Ralph Bunche School ("The world's first elementary school")

1. About the Ralph Bunche School
2. Search Titles On The RBS Gopher <?>
3. Recent Ralph Bunche School newspaper stories/
4. Shadows Science Project/
5. Student Work/
6. Junior High School 43/
7. RBS Goes to NECC 94/
8. FCC Chair Reed Hundt Visits RBS/
9. Student Introductions/
10. BBN's National School Network Testbed/
11. Information about GN, a gopher/WWW server/
12. RBS.GIF <Picture>

In item #2, the <?> symbol indicates that this option permits subject searches by keyword. By selecting this choice, you have the opportunity to enter a search, or key, word.

Let's select this option. This is the screen that appears:

< 64 >

```
        Search Titles On The RBS Gopher
             Words to search for
         [Help: ^-] [Cancel: ^G]
```

Now let's enter our keyword **computers** .

```
        Search Titles On The RBS Gopher
             Words to search for
                 computers
         [Help: ^-] [Cancel: ^G]
```

Here is the menu that appears:

Search Titles On The RBS Gopher: computer

1. Junior Sysop Study Computers (Shaun Santana & Anthony Phillips)
2. Students Help Teachers On Computers
3. Two kids from 36 enjoy the computer <Picture>
4. Classroom gets New Computers
5. Computer Room Floor Gets Fixed
6. Computer Technology at RBS
7. News About the Ralph Bunche Computer School

Notice that every item in this menu contains the word "computer" somewhere in its title. This new menu was custom-made for us. It gives us a good place to begin reading about what Ralph Bunche Elementary School does with computers.

Not every keyword that you choose will result in a

< 65 >

search. If we chose the keyword "homework," for instance, we get this result:

```
              Gopher Error
              Nothing available
              [Cancel: ^G] [OK:
```

▶TIP Although the style of search commands varies slightly from one kind of Gopher program to another, your search strategy and your search results will look the same no matter what kind of gopher program you are using.

SEARCHING THROUGH GOPHERSPACE

There will be many times when you approach Gopherspace looking for information related to a specific topic. You might be working on a school paper. You might be exploring a career interest. Or you might have a question related to your hobby or sport. Browsing might be a good way to begin such research, but very quickly you will want to search Gopherspace in a more systematic, productive manner.

To do this, you'll need to use a Gopher search tool called Veronica. Veronica is a program that searches through the menus in Gopherspace for a specific keyword. Veronica will present to you a menu listing resources related to your search word.

WHY THE NAME VERONICA? Veronica supposedly stands for Very Easy Rodent-Oriented Net-wide Index to Computerized Archives. Does that sound like a rather contrived name? Veronica also

< 66 >

happens to be the name of a character from the Archie comics. Is it a coincidence that Archie is another type of Internet search tool? (Actually Archie was developed first. Not until Veronica came along were the names of the search tools linked to the names of the comic book characters.)

A keyword search with Veronica is very similar to the type of keyword search you did earlier with the Ralph Bunche Elementary School Gopher. Some important differences exist, however. In the keyword search, you looked through one Gopher server, the Ralph Bunche Elementary School Gopher. A Veronica search examines all the hundreds of Gopher servers around the world in its search for menu titles that contain your keyword. Veronica also allows you to focus your search in a variety of ways.

SAMPLE SEARCHES WITH VERONICA

Let's suppose you want to use Gopher to find information for a research report about students bringing guns to school. You decide to run a keyword search with Veronica. To start, you will need to find a Gopher menu selection for Veronica. Look for Veronica in your main menu's selection choices. If you're having trouble finding Veronica, look for menu items with titles like "Finding information" or "Searching titles in Gopherspace" or even "Internet services."

Once you find Veronica, you're ready to start your search. You decide to search on the keyword "gun". Type **gun** into the Veronica option. (Always press Enter after Veronica commands.) This is the first page of the multipage menu that results.

< 67 >

1. Gun-in-home?-Study-finds-it-a-deadly-mix.
2. Forestry under the gun: An evaluation of SIDA-supported forestry
3. HB0054 Tax Credit for Gun Safes
4. Gun Control Information/
5. CBS NEWS "48 HOURS" GUN POLL, MARCH 1989
6. gun.txt. [06-Apr 15:04:48, 5KB]
7. Gun Control Petition
8. Gun Control Petition
9. Re: AER article and redistribution at the point of a gun
10. Gun Safety Courses Offered
11. 94-07-11-19: PSR: Gun Violence Symposium
12. 94-06-29-01: Gun Violence Symposium
13. Gun Safety
14. Ohio favorite for gun traffic
15. Gun control does not inhibit hunting
16. Letters: Gun control
17. Letters: Gun lover
18. Criminals not solely to blame for gun problem

Page: 1/12

You can see from the first screen that your search turned up twelve pages of items. That sounds like a lot—until you reach the last item, #200 on page 12. Another 1,099 items are available! It looks like this:

Keyword Search - Worldwide Menus - Titles: gun

199. Re: 30 shots fired... This country is gun crazy... [20] wagner@ch..

200. * * There are 1099 more items matching the query "gun" available* *

< 68 >

This highlights a feature of Veronica. Don't count on it to give you everything it finds. Veronica cuts off its search after the first 200 items it finds.

Now you need to narrow your search. Try **gun and school**. This will result in a search for items that contain both terms. Using **and** narrows a search.

Keyword Search - Worldwide Menus - Titles :
gun and school

1. School Prayer, Gun Control and the Righ
2. Modern Gun Repair School
3. Gun Free School Act Ruled Okay (2k)
4. Gun Free School Act 1990 (5k)

Only four items were found. Although these items look interesting, the search is now too narrow. There must be more than four relevant documents in Gopherspace. You decide to broaden your search by using a more general keyword than "gun." You try **weapon and school**.

Keyword Search - Worldwide Menus - Titles :
weapon and school

1. Weapon-Free School Zones 10/94

Only one item? That's much too narrow. At this point you need to figure out how to broaden your search while still staying close to your topic. You decide to try **safe and school**.

< 69 >

Keyword Search - Worldwide Menus - Titles :
safe and school

1. SCR003 Resolution Endorsing Safe School Community
2. SAFE SCHOOL STUDY, 1976-1977
3. Safe School Plan
4. Safe School Study, 1976-1977
5. 95-03-28 Providing a Safe Drug-Free School Environment
6. America's Safe School Week: tips for prevention
7. America's Safe School Week: tips for prevention
8. America's Safe School Week: tips for prevention
9. The Safe School Act of 1994 and GOALS 2000
10. Safe at School: Awareness & Action for Parents...
    (Saunders)/
11. Safe School Study, 1976-1977
12. Safe School Study, 1976-1977
Page: 1/1

Twelve items—that's better. But then you wonder whether "safety" might be a better search term than "safe." You run a search with **safety and school**.

Keyword Search - Worldwide Menus - Titles :
safety and school

1. HB0022 School Zone Safety Speed
2. HB0022 School Zone Safety Speed
3. Tennessee School Health and Safety Profile
4. re: grad school in radiological safety (health physics)
5. Missouri School Improvement Facilities and Safety
   (Sec. 14)
6. School Safety Plan
7. School Safety
8. RE: School Safety Plan

< 70 >

9. Re: School Safety Workshop
10. Re: School Safety
11. School Safety
12. Re: School Safety
13. RE: School Safety
14: Re: School Safety
15. School Earthquake Safety Information
16. "School/Pedestrian Safety"
17. 09-03-94 School Safety
18. Primary Safety: On the Way to School
Page: 1/2

Now you have two pages of items. You're happy with the results of this search. But this list is missing the documents you found with the "safe and school" search. Is there a way to combine the two searches? Yes—by using an asterisk (*) to replace the letters at the end of a word. The search term "safe*" will turn up documents that contain both "safe" and "safety." (A keyword with an asterisk in it is known as a wild card.) Your new search is **safe* and school**.

Keyword Search - Worldwide Menus - Titles :
safe* and school

1. HB0022 School Zone Safety Speed
2. SCR003 Resolution Endorsing Safe School Community
3. HB0022 School Zone Safety Speed
4. SAFE SCHOOL STUDY, 1976-1977
5. Tennessee School Health and Safety Profile
6. re: grad school in radiological safety (health physics)
7. Missouri School Improvement Facilities and Safety (Sec. 14)
8. School Safety Plan
9. School Safety
10. RE: School Safety Plan

< 71 >

11. Safe School Plan
12. Re: School Safety Workshop
13. Re: School Safety
14. School Safety
15. Re: School Safety
16. RE: School Safety
17. Re: School Safety
18. School Earthquake Safety Information
Page: 1/3

You can feel confident now that you have all the items related to "safe" and "safety" and "school." A quick glance tells you that not all of the items are relevant to your topic, but this is a broad enough listing to get you started.

What if you decide that even this list is too long? Perhaps you want to see only major holdings of items related to school safety. You can do this by adding another command **(-t1)** to the keyword search. The command **-t1** is a request to see only menus, not single documents. (There are other **-t** commands. You can read about them in Internet guides that go into more detail about Veronica.)

Type **safe* and school -t1** to see only a list of menus related to gun control. (You know that an item is a menu if it is followed by a forward slash.) This list is quite short:

Keyword Search - Worldwide Menus - Titles :
safe* and school -t1

1. School Safety/
2. School Safety/
3. Safe at School: Awareness & Action for Parents...
    (Saunders)/

< 72 >

In this example, the search started very broadly, and various features of Veronica were used to narrow it. Sometimes the opposite happens. Let's suppose you're beginning research on ocean pollution. You tell Veronica to search **ocean pollution**. (You could also write this command as **ocean and pollution**.) This is the menu that appears:

Keyword Search - Worldwide Menus - Titles :
ocean pollution

1. 93-11-12-16: Ocean pollution
2. 93-11-18-04: Re: Ocean pollution
3. Researchers measure ocean pollution
4. Sources for Ocean Pollution Project ?
5. Re: Sources for Ocean Pollution Project
6. Ocean pollution database
7. An Assessment of Great Lakes and Ocean Pollution
    Monitoring in the

Page: 1/1

This is too narrow. You decide to broaden your topic to everything under ocean pollution and lake pollution. You can use parentheses to do this. You command Veronica to search for **pollution (ocean or lake)**. Using **or** results in a search for items that contain the word "pollution" and either "ocean" or "lake." Using **or** broadens a search.

Keyword Search - Worldwide Menus - Titles : pollution
(ocean or lake)

1. Lake Michigan Toxic Pollution Control/ Reduction
   Strategy

< 73 >

2. Water Pollution Problems of Lake Michigan and Its Tributaries
3. Conference in the Matter of Pollution of Lake Michigan
4. Conference in the Matter of Pollution of Lake Michigan
5. Conference in the Matter of Pollution of Lake Michigan
6. Ocean pollution databases
7. Lake Michigan toxic pollution control/reduction
8. Researchers measure ocean pollution
9. 93-11-18-04: Re: Ocean pollution
10. Lake Michigan Pollution and Chicago's Supply
11. Report of the Panel on Water Supply, Lake Pollution, and Lake Level
12. Lake-Effect Snowfall and Some Implications for. . .
13. Comprehensive Water Pollution Control Pro-gram for Lake Michigan
14. 93-11-12-16: Ocean pollution
15. Study Pinpoints Lake Pollution
16. A Report on Pollution of Lake Michigan in the Vicinity of Chicago's. . .
17. Lake Michigan toxic pollution control/reduction
18. CAM: Pollution threatens Cambodia's largest lake
Page: 1/3

The results of this search—three pages of items—gives you a good place to begin. But let's suppose you would rather not see items about Lake Michigan. You can use **not** to eliminate those items from your search. You command Veronica to search **pollution (ocean or lake) not Michigan**. The use of **not** narrows a search. This is the result of that search:

Keyword Search - Worldwide Menus - Titles :
pollution (ocean or lake) not Michigan

1. Ocean pollution databases
2. Researchers measure ocean pollution

< 74 >

3. 93-11-18-04: Re: Ocean pollution
4. Report of the Panel on Water Supply, Lake Pollution, and Lake Level
5. Lake-Effect Snowfall and Some Implications for. . .
6. 93-11-12-16: Ocean pollution
7. Study Pinpoints Lake Pollution
8. CAM: Pollution threatens Cambodia's largest lake
9. An Assessment of Great Lakes and Ocean Pollution Monitoring
10. Lake Michigan Pollution and Chicago's Supply
11. Trajectory Analyses of Mesoscale Air Pollution Transport
12. Report of the Panel on Water Supply, Lake Pollution, and Lake Level
13. Re: Sources for Ocean Pollution Project
14. Water Quality in the Calumet Area: Conference on Pollution of. . .
15. Mesoscale Air Pollution Transport in the Chicago Lake Breeze
16. Water Pollution Control and Abatement, Part 3, Chicago Area and. . .
17. Lake Effects on Air Pollution Dispersion
18. Report to Pollution Probe/Lake Ontario Organizing

Page: 1/2

KEYWORD SEARCH STRATEGIES

1. Choose your keyword carefully. You may want to try several different keywords to see what yields the best results.

2. Use an asterisk to replace the letters in a word to get several forms of the word.

    safe* = safe and safety

3. You can use several keywords combined with **and**, **or**, and **not**. If two words appear next to each other, Veronica assumes that they are joined by and.

< 75 >

4. You can write and, or, and not in uppercase and lowercase.
5. To narrow a search, use and or not.
6. To broaden a search, use or.
7. If your search contains several keywords and more than one logical operator (**and**, **or**, **not**), use parentheses.

pollution (ocean or lake)

8. By using the -**t1** command you can limit your search to only items that are menus. You can put this command before or after your keyword.

SAVING GOPHER FILES

What if you want to actually obtain some of the items you find? In the library, you can photocopy articles. In Gopherspace, you can capture the items you find and send them to your computer.

You have a choice of printing them out, sending them to yourself by e-mail, or transferring them directly to your own computer's directory. Not all methods are possible on all computer systems. Ask your teacher which method is best for your school's computer system.

COMMANDS TO USE WITH UNIX GOPHER PROGRAMS

Command	Function
m	Mail
s	Save
p	Print
D	Download

< 76 >

The next chapter discusses another useful Internet feature. This feature allows you to move documents, pictures, and other kinds of information kept on computer files from a distant computer to your home computer. This feature is called ftp: file transfer protocol.

< 77 >

MOVING FILES:
FILE TRANSFER PROTOCOL

Gopher is one source of information in cyberspace. Another good place to find information is among the files of other computers connected to the Internet. Computer files can contain text documents, like those you see with Gopher. Files can also contain useful computer programs, computer games, and pictures.

Many computer sites on the Internet have vast numbers of computer files kept in a storage area called an archive. Most sites are private, of course, and offer access only to authorized users. But other sites make it possible for anyone on the Internet to enter their archives and make copies of the files they want for free. These sites are called "anonymous ftp sites." (FTP stands for "file transfer protocol.")

If you are new to computers, you might not have an immediate need for file transfer protocol. As you become

< 79 >

more familiar with computers, however, you will begin hearing about interesting computer files. You might read in a newsgroup or a book or a magazine article about a document you can obtain with ftp. A friend might tell you about a game that she downloaded from an anonymous ftp site. At that point, you'll be ready to try ftp.

Here are the basic steps for using ftp:

1. First, determine whether ftp is available through your computer system. At the main prompt, type **ftp** and press Enter. If the next prompt looks like this: **ftp>**, then you know this feature is available to you. To return to the main prompt, type **quit**.

2. Before you can move a specific file to your computer system, you need to know the name of the file, the address of the anonymous ftp site where the file is located, and the directory in which the file is stored. Many files are available at more than one site.

In this example, the file **soc.feminism_Information** will be retrieved. It contains information about the newsgroup **soc.feminism** and is recommended reading for anyone new to that group. (See Chapter Three for more about newsgroups.)

The file will be retrieved from an anonymous ftp site that contains newsgroup FAQs and other information posted periodically for people new to newsgroups. Although this newsgroup information originates at **rtfm.mit.edu**, located at the Massachusetts Institute of Technology, it is also made available at other sites, including **ftp.seas.gwu.edu**, at George Washington University. That is the site used in this example.

The file is in the directory **/pub/rtfm/soc/feminism/** .

3. Now you are ready to make a connection between your computer system and the remote site. At your system's main prompt, type **ftp** followed by a space and then the site name. Press Enter.

< 80 >

ftp ftp.seas.gwu.edu

4. You will see a confirmation that the connection was made. Then you will be asked for your name. Type **anonymous**. Press Enter.

5. When asked for your password, type your full e-mail address (or you may be prompted to type **guest**). Press Enter. You will not be able to see what you type in as your password.

6. At the prompt **ftp>** type **cd** followed by a space and then the directory name:

ftp> cd /pub/rtfm/soc/feminism/

You will see a confirmation, **CWD command successful**.

7. Type the command **dir** to list the contents of that directory. Press Enter. This is what you will see:

```
drwxr-xr-x   2 root    root    512 Nov 3 09:46 .
drwxr-xr-x  18 root    root    512 Nov 10 09:49 .
-r—r—r—     1 root    root    23673 Nov 3 06:55 soc.feminism_Information
-r—r—r—     1 root    root    67889 Nov 3 06:55 soc.feminism_References_(part_1_of_3)
-r—r—r—     1 root    root    25926 Nov 3 06:55 soc.feminism_References_(part_2_of_3)
-r—r—r—     1 root    root    45396 Nov 3 06:55 soc.feminism_References_(part_3_of_3)
-r—r—r—     1 root    root    64701 Nov 3 06:56 soc.feminism_Resources
-r—r—r—     1 root    root    35269 Nov 3 06:56 soc.feminism_Terminologies
```

Each line in a directory contains information on a particular file or subdirectory. Look to the end of the line for the names of files and subdirectories. The information in the middle of the line includes the size of the file or subdirectory and the date it was created.

< 81 >

At the beginning of the line is an odd collection of letters and dashes. A line that begins with a dash (-) indicates a file that can be transferred. A line that begins with a "d" is a subdirectory that contains another list of files and subdirectories.

8. Check and see that the file you want is in the directory. Now you're ready to send it to your computer system. At the prompt **ftp** type **get** followed by a space and then the file name. Press Enter.

ftp> get soc.feminism_Information

9. You will be given a report on the size of the file sent and the time it took to transfer it. When the transfer is over, you will see the prompt **ftp** again. Here's what it looks like:

```
200 PORT command successful.
150 Opening ASCII mode data connection for soc.
    feminism_Information (23673 bytes).
226 Transfer complete.
local: soc.feminism_Information remote:
    soc.feminism_Information
24125 bytes received in 0.82 seconds (29 Kbytes/s)
ftp>
```

10. To disconnect, type **quit**. Press Enter. The remote system will say **goodbye** and then you will be back at your own system's prompt.

11. Although the file is now in your own computer system, you will probably need to download it with a special program. Check with your teacher to discover the best way to download the file. If you have a UNIX system, you can type the command **ls** at the system prompt to double-check that the file arrived.

< 82 >

OTHER FTP FEATURES

Moving Through Directories

At ftp sites, one directory may be subdivided into many subdirectories and each of *those* subdirectories might be divided into even more subdirectories. That's why it is very useful to know the precise subdirectory of the file you want. (In this example, **soc.feminism_Information** was found within a subdirectory called **feminism** within a subdirectory called **soc** within a subdirectory called **rtfm** within a directory called **pub**.)

If you don't know the precise location of a file, however, or if you merely want to investigate the holdings of a particular ftp site, commands exist that give you some control over the various levels of directories. Commands are typed at the prompt **ftp.**

pwd	Reveals the name of the directory you are in ("pwd" stands for print working directory)
dir	Reveals the contents (files and subdirectories) of the directory you are in
cd <new directory name>	Changes directories
cd ../..	Changes directories; moves up one level to previous subdirectory
quit	Exits system

Reading Files

You can also read the contents of a file while you are connected to a ftp site. In fact, in the first directory at a ftp site you may see a file named README. This file contains useful information about the contents of the ftp site. At the prompt **ftp** type **get** followed by a space, the file name, another space, and ¦ **more.** (That broken vertical line is called a "pipe.")

< 83 >

ftp> get soc.feminism_Information ¦ more

The text of the document will follow. Use the spacebar to page through it.

Changing File Names

If the file name provided by the ftp site is too long or awkward, you can change it when you move the file to your computer system. At the prompt **ftp** type **get** followed by a space, the file name, another space, and your new name for the file. Here's is what you'll see:

```
ftp> get soc.feminism_Information new_name
200 PORT command successful.
150 Opening ASCII mode data connection for soc.
    feminism_Information (23673 bytes).
226 Transfer complete.
local: new_name remote: soc.feminism_Information
24125 bytes received in 1.1 seconds (22 Kbytes/s)
```

Moving Nontext Files

In cyberspace, pictures are known as "binaries" or "binary images." Before moving nontext files, like pictures, at the **ftp** prompt type **image**. At the next prompt you'll be ready to order your transfer.

ARCHIE

Archie is an Internet search tool that locates the archive location of particular files. Archie earned its name by dropping the "v" from "archive."

Look for a full description of Archie in a longer, more detailed guide to the Internet. (See the Resources section.) Briefly, there are several ways to connect to Archie.

< 84 >

Your computer system may run an Archie program. Archie can also be reached through telnet, Gopher, the World Wide Web (see Chapter Seven), and even e-mail.

To use Archie, you will need to type in the name of the file you're searching for. If you're conducting a general search, Archie offers several different search strategies. An Archie search will turn up a list of files and where to find them. You will then need to use anonymous ftp to actually retrieve the files.

< 85 >

THE WORLD WIDE WEB

Imagine the Internet as a place, a vast world of written messages and documents, and sometimes pictures and even sound. Now imagine it as several parallel universes. Electronic mail is one universe. Newsgroups are another universe. Gopher is yet another. It's not completely correct to think of them as separate universes, of course, since often you can move from one to the other very easily. But when you consider the kind of information they offer and the way you work within each of them, they do seem rather different.

This chapter describes another universe, one known as the World Wide Web. The Web is like your favorite magazine, your favorite television program, and your favorite class at school all rolled into one. It's a place to browse for information and entertainment. Have you

< 87 >

ever browsed? Perhaps you've thumbed through a thick magazine or skimmed the newspaper, or dipped in and out of a photo album, looking at whatever pictures caught your eye. If you have lots of television stations, you've probably spent some time channel-surfing.

Browsing the Web is so easy and so much fun that it's a lot like channel-surfing. In fact, many people talk about surfing the Web (and surfing the Net). Although the Web is an information source, like Gopher, most people think it's more fun than Gopher.

The Web links together thousands of different information sources from around the globe. (Think of the way the strands of a spider web cross and connect.) These information sources contain text—and pictures, sound, and even video. The pictures, in fact, are usually what people think of when they think of the Web. What kind of pictures? You name it: faces, fossils, photographs, drawings, satellite images and pictures of coloring book pages are all available on the Web.

Unfortunately, not everybody with access to the Web is going to be able to see the pictures. To explore the Web, you need a special kind of computer program known as a Web browser. Many browsers are designed to show graphics but some show only text. Although this sounds disappointing, it can actually be good news. It means even computers that are unable to handle fancy, full-color graphics can still be used to browse a text-only version of the Web.

Dozens of Web browsers exist. Mosaic, Netscape, and InternetWorks are three popular browsers that allow you to see pictures and text. Lynx is a browser that reveals only text. With any browser, you can navigate the Web easily, keep track of the information sites you visit, and save what you find. Each type of browser, however, uses a different set of commands to carry out those functions. In this chapter, we'll explore in a general way how the

< 88 >

two basic types of browsers work. To learn about all the available browsers and the commands they use, you'll need to consult a book specifically about the World Wide Web.

Information on the Web is organized into Web documents. One document contains screens of information filled with words and pictures, and sometimes also sound and video. Documents can be very short (one screen) or very long (many screens). Web documents are also called Web pages.

Here's what a sample Web page looks like:

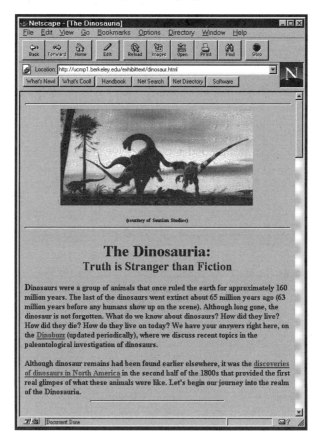

< 89 >

Netscape, a browser that lets you see graphics, is the browser used here.

Now look at the same Web page with Lynx, a text-based browser:

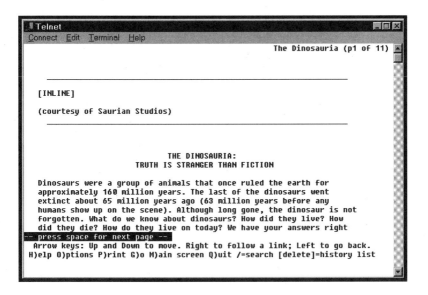

Instead of the actual images, a text-only browser shows the word ["INLINE"].

You can clearly see the difference. Lynx shows only the words, while Netscape shows both the words and the images in the Web document.

Here are some more Web pages, as seen with Netscape:

< 90 >

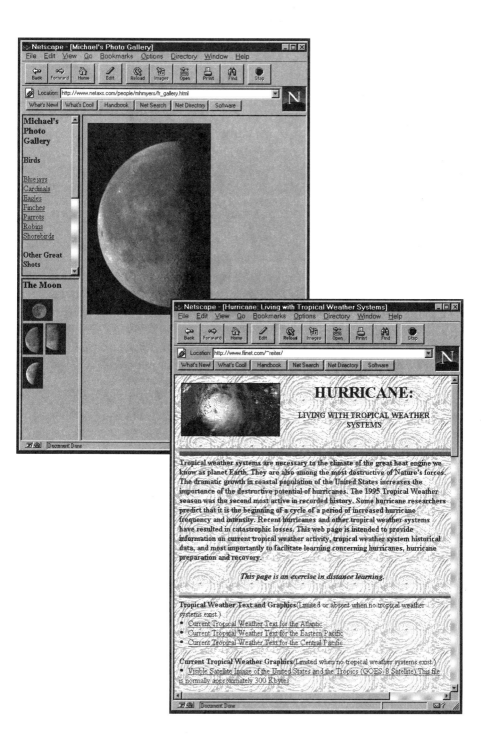

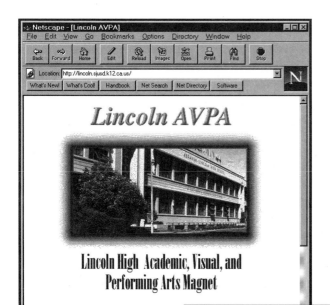

Netscape - [Lincoln AVPA]

File   Edit   View   Go   Bookmarks   Options   Directory   Window   Help

Back | Forward | Home | Edit | Reload | Images | Open | Print | Find | Stop

Location: http://lincoln.sjusd.k12.ca.us/

What's New! | What's Cool! | Handbook | Net Search | Net Directory | Software

Lincoln AVPA

Lincoln High Academic, Visual, and Performing Arts Magnet

Welcome to Lincoln Hi

555 Dana Avenu
San Jose, California
USA

(408) 535-6300

Abraham Lincoln High has bee

Document: Done

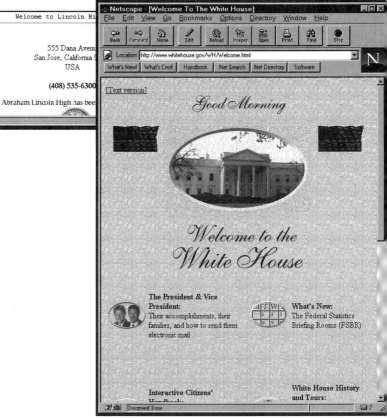

Netscape - [Welcome To The White House]

File   Edit   View   Go   Bookmarks   Options   Directory   Window   Help

Back | Forward | Home | Edit | Reload | Images | Open | Print | Find | Stop

Location: http://www.whitehouse.gov/WH/Welcome.html

What's New! | What's Cool! | Handbook | Net Search | Net Directory | Software

[Text version]

Good Morning

Welcome to the
White House

The President & Vice President:
Their accomplishments, their families, and how to send them electronic mail

What's New:
The Federal Statistics Briefing Rooms (FSBR)

Interactive Citizens'

White House History and Tours:

Document: Done

So what? you might be thinking. These screen shots are fun to look at but what's the big deal? An encyclopedia has text and pictures, and I already know how to use an encyclopedia. What's so special about the Web?

Good question. One reason the Web is so special—and so exciting—is that it contains an incredible variety of material. Some of it is scholarly but much of it has to do with sports, cartoons, music, movies, fashion, and fun. The Web is filled with details about contemporary events and pop culture—much more so than an encyclopedia or Gopher. You can find stuff about the Grateful Dead and the late Jerry Garcia, Star Trek, the Simpsons, and Calvin & Hobbes here. In addition, the Web is full of pages created by interesting people to introduce and describe themselves. Hundreds of high schools have Web pages filled with photos of students and teachers.

The way you move through a Web site is also what makes the Web unique. There is no single, obvious way to read through a Web site. Web sites are created so that you jump from one part of the document to another by following links.

Links are like buttons you click on with your computer mouse to jump from one document to another. A link is usually several highlighted words. If you're viewing a Web page about upcoming Hollywood movies, and you run across the highlighted name "Keanu Reeves," you can click on the name and immediately be presented with a screenful of information about that actor. Pictures and menu options can also be links. (If you've ever used a book on a CD, it's like that.)

At any time while reading, you can select a link and move to another portion of the document. Links allow you to move through a document in your own fashion. You may follow a path of exploration that no one else would choose. That's one of the attractions of the Web: it allows you to create your own path of discovery.

< 93 >

WHAT IS A HOME PAGE? This expression has come to have two meanings. The first page that appears when you go to a Web document is called its home page. The first page that appears when you start your Web browser is *your* home page.

The pages of a Web document contain links to other pages within the same document. Every document is also connected through links to other Web documents. One way of thinking of the Web, in fact, is as a single, gigantic document.

Let's follow some links through the World Wide Web. Here's a Web document from NASA. Notice the highlighted topics to choose from.

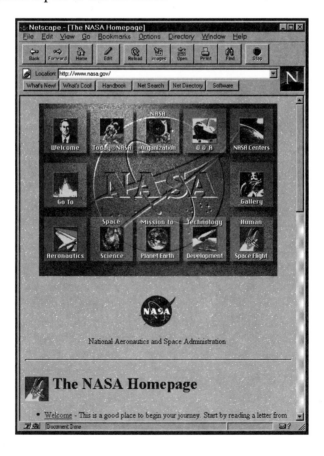

Now let's click on "Human Space Flight," one of the highlighted topics. This screen appears:

Using links is slightly different with the text-based browsers. With Lynx, you'll use the arrow keys or tab key to move between highlighted links. With the Line Mode browser, links are shown with a number in brackets. To choose a link, you must type a number and press the Enter key.

USING WEB ADDRESSES

Browsing the Web is fun and turns up all kinds of exciting things. But what do you do if you read in a

< 95 >

magazine about a specific Web site that you really want to see?

You can go immediately to any Web document you wish, provided that you know its Internet address. Remember, addresses of documents and files on the Internet are known as Uniform Resource Locators, or URLs for short. Here's the Uniform Resource Leader for the World Wide Web Hall of Fame:

http://wings.buffalo.edu/contest/awards/fame.html

A World Wide Web URL almost always starts with the letters **http**. This stands for HyperText Transfer Protocol. (A document that is connected to other documents via links is known as "hypertext.") A URL often also contains the letters **www**, for World Wide Web. The next part of the address tells something about the organization that created the page: **wings.buffalo.edu**. This site was created by an educational institution (the University of Buffalo). The words separated by slashes show the names of the pages that lead to the web document. Last of all are often the letters **html**, which make it clear that this is hypertext, created by using HyperText Markup Language, the simple code used to write Web pages.

▶ **T I P** Web addresses are partially case-sensitive. For best results, always type in the URL exactly as it appears.

When you visit a Web document, your computer screen will display its URL. This will be the only way to learn a document's URL if you have used links to travel to it. Obviously, if you find a document you wish to return to easily, it is useful to know its URL. See if you can spot the URL of the World Wide Web Hall of Fame:

< 96 >

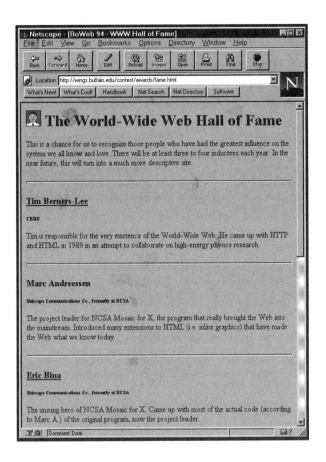

But you don't have to keep an address book of URLs just to keep track of your journeys through the Web. Your Web browser is set up to allow you to create a list of Web documents you visit frequently. (This list may be called a "hotlist" or "bookmark," depending upon your browser.) That's where you put your favorite sites, so you can easily return to them again and again.

You can also keep track of a single session's journey on the Web. Backward and forward keys let you move back to sites you've just left behind and then forward again. A feature known as a "history list" catalogs all the sites you've visited in a single session (also known as

< 97 >

a "card catalog" or "document trail," depending upon your browser).

FUN WEB SITES TO VISIT! See the Internet Resources section for a list of Web sites worth visiting. Start your own list by recording the URLs you see mentioned in magazines, newspapers, newsgroups, and other Internet books. Ask your friends, too.

WEB DIRECTORIES

At times you'll want to use the Web to find material on a specific subject, maybe for a school project. Several Web directories index material on the Web. They not only give you the names and addresses (URLs) of documents, but they also provide links to those Web sites. Needless to say, these directories are the best place to start when using the Web for research. Here are some well-known Web directories. More are springing up all the time.

Yahoo Directory

http://www.yahoo.com/

MetaCrawler

http://metacrawler.cs.washington.edu:8080/index.html/

WWW Virtual Library

http://www.w3.org/hypertext/DataSources/bySubject/Overview.html

WebCrawler Searching

http://webcrawler.com/

InfoSeek Guide

http://www.infoseek.com/

< 98 >

Lycos Home Page
http://lycos.cs.cmu.edu/

Alta Vista

http://www.altavista.digital.com/
Alta Vista conducts keyword searches on the World Wide Web.

Femina

http://www.femina.com/

Femina is a directory of women's resources on the Web.

Learn these basic commands for your particular Web browser:

How to follow links.
How to move backward and forward during a session.
How to use the history list.
How to use the hotlist feature.
How to save a Web document: download, mail, or print.

< 99 >

COLLABORATING THROUGH THE INTERNET

The Internet is a tool that can put you in touch with hundreds, thousands, even millions of people. One of the unique features of the Internet is the way it enables people to communicate directly with many other people. This type of communication is different from the telephone, which is one person to one person. It's also different from television or radio, which broadcasts one program to many people.

You can use the power of the Internet to carry out projects with people scattered across the world. You can also use it to share the stories, artwork, and articles you create. You can even enrich the Net itself by building new resources, like a Web site or a Gopher server.

This chapter and the next will look at real-life exam-

< 101 >

ples of how students and teachers are using the Internet to communicate and collaborate. This is a sampling of different types of activities. Some of them can be done with only e-mail access. Others require access to the World Wide Web. For more information on these projects, or to join a project that's right for your school, explore the Internet Resources section of this book.

CALL FOR ACTION

On the twenty-fifth anniversary of Earth Day, April 22, 1995, thousands of shoppers in the United States and Canada were reminded by the artwork of children to use the Earth's resources wisely. Schoolchildren in towns across the United States and Canada had embellished plain brown grocery bags from local supermarkets with pictures of the Earth, the words "Earth Day 1995," and other slogans. After the bags were decorated, they were returned to the stores and used to pack the groceries of people shopping on Earth Day.

What an easy way to celebrate this important anniversary! It all started in 1994 when Arbor Heights Elementary School in Seattle, Washington, used the Internet to encourage schools across the country to take part in the Earth Day Grocery Bag Project. That year, over 13,000 grocery bags in the United States and Canada were decorated. The number tripled in 1995, when 44,619 bags were made.

< 102 >

Great local projects can make great international projects. If you have a good idea for a local community activity, consider spreading the word and making a global statement by using e-mail, newsgroups, and mailing lists. Activities like the Earth Day Grocery Bag Project are extremely easy to initiate. They require no organization, no central headquarters, and no sponsorship. If it's a good idea, it will travel fast on the Internet.

STUDENT SCIENTISTS

Students who live far apart can use the Internet to put their heads together and make sense out of what each one is seeing. An observation that seems relatively insignificant—the sighting of the first robin in the spring, for instance—can suddenly take on larger meaning when it is combined with the sightings of spring robins by many people across the continent.

You and other student scientists can use the almost instantaneous communication of the Internet to compare research notes and draw conclusions about such large-scale phenomena as animal and butterfly migration, air pollution, acid rain, and the coming of spring. You can also use it to compare aspects of daily life, like the cost of groceries.

Here are some examples of data-collecting projects.

Journey North

This ambitious project asked students across North America to report their sightings of monarch butterflies, bald eagles, songbirds, peregrine

< 103 >

falcons, caribou, loons, and other species to a central e-mail address. These reports were then distributed via Gopher and the World Wide Web. By pooling their observations, students studied the movements and migration of many species. This activity was sponsored in part by Minneapolis-based Hamline University's Center for Global Environmental Education.

Acid Rain Project

In this project, students around the world collected rainwater and measured its acidity level. Their discoveries were shared with other classes through e-mail. A collaboration of fifteen classes around the world, organized by a school in Sharon, Massachusetts, carried out this activity. The students learned that acid levels were much lower in rural areas than in cities.

Global Grocery List

In this project, students around the world visit their local grocery store with a short shopping list that includes oranges, milk, coffee, chicken, hamburger, and rice. They record the price of the groceries and then send their results to a central e-mail address. The information is shared with other students around the world via a mailing list. It is also stored on a World Wide Web page. The information can be used in science, health, math, and social studies classes. This activity is sponsored by the Global School-Net Foundation.

In these types of projects, many people share their observations and data. Sometimes they then work

< 104 >

together to make sense of those observations. Such activities require more organization and coordination than something like the Earth Day Grocery Bag Project. They seem to work best if a central headquarters takes responsibility for collecting all the data and making it available to everyone.

JOIN A JOURNEY

Did you ever wonder what it would be like to journey by dogsled across the North Pole? Or to excavate the site of an ancient civilization? Or travel by balloon across the United States? What about joining another class as it visits a local historical site or business? You can use the Internet to join the journeys of other people.

Here are some sample journeys:

Fieldtrips Project Mailing List

Is your class planning to visit a historical battlefield? Attend a Broadway play? Volunteer at a food pantry? Share the experience over the Internet with other classes. The Global SchoolNet Foundation will help you select a partner class for the trip. Your partner class will ask you questions about your field trip and you will act as their eyes and ears as you make the trip. You can also use the foundation's mailing list to become a partner to a class making a trip.

International Arctic Project

Polar explorer Will Steger and an international team of two women and three men traveled across the surface of the frozen Arctic Ocean by

< 105 >

dogsled and canoe-sled in 1995. This expedition was sponsored in part by the Scholastic Network on America Online.

MayaQuest

In 1995, a team of bicyclists traveled through Guatemala, Mexico, Belize, and Honduras, where they visited archaeologists investigating the ruins of the ancient Mayan civilization. This journey had several sponsors, including Internet for Minnesota Schools (InforMNs) and Prodigy.

Balloonin' USA

During the 1995-96 school year, school superintendent and balloon pilot Kevin Kuehn traveled by hot-air balloon across the United States. Along the way, Kuehn took measurements of barometric pressure, precipitation, and wind speed. He reported on what he found at the schools where his balloon touched down. Classrooms across the country communicated with him through e-mail and the World Wide Web.

Be sure to find ways to make these journeys your own. Unless it is your class making the trip, as in the Fieldtrips Project Mailing List, you are being placed in the position of observer and invited to watch someone else's adventure. This tends to make this type of project less collaborative than other Internet projects. Take advantage of opportunities to ask the explorers questions or make suggestions regarding their itinerary. You might want to think about the journey reports as raw, unedited material that you must shape into news stories.

< 106 >

INVESTIGATING PLANET EARTH

For years, satellites orbiting the Earth collected thousands of photographs of the planet. Thanks to the Internet, those images are now available to everyone, including students. This wide distribution of satellite-collected data has made a new field of study possible: Earth systems science.

Earth systems science examines how different systems of the Earth—including the oceans, atmosphere, and living creatures—interact. The discipline pulls together biology, chemistry, oceanography, geology, and other research areas into one program of study. In a NASA-sponsored program, Gonzaga College High School in Spokane, Washington, and seven other high schools in the United States and Canada are using the satellite data to develop and answer research questions. Their project is known as the Earth Systems Science Curriculum Community.

Although the Earth Systems Science Curriculum Community is a unique project, it shows the kind of collaborations that Internet information can make possible. Encourage your teacher to look for other projects like this one.

WRITING WITH OTHERS

Did you ever ask for ideas as you were writing a story or report? Or ask for feedback when you were done? Have you ever written a story with another person? Consider tapping into the expertise of the Internet to launch writing collaborations or to garner feedback for what you have written.

< 107 >

Here's how two schools used the Internet for their writing projects:

Collaborative Fiction

Students in Tom Keeler's class at Project City Elementary School in Shasta Lake, California, used the Internet to create fiction stories with kids around the world. They sent story starters to classrooms connected to the Internet and asked students to write the next paragraph of the story. After this was done, the story was sent back to California where it was then redirected to another classroom for another paragraph. In this manner the elementary class created hundreds of stories, some of which have traveled around the world.

Essay Feedback

If you visit the Web pages of North Hagerstown High School in Washington County, Maryland, you can read many student essays written for social studies class. (Web address: **http://www.fred.net/nhhs/nhhs.html**) Topics for the first set of essays included "The President as Hero or Anti-Hero" and "Martin Luther King's Dream and the Reality of Black America." Visitors to the Web site are invited to provide feedback to the student authors. Reviewers are specifically invited to offer constructive criticism regarding the historical content and structure of the essays. The guest reviewers are also asked to discuss how sources were used and documented.

You don't need a web site to do this activity. The students at North Hagerstown High School ini-

< 108 >

tially sent their essays by e-mail to volunteer readers. Their teacher, George Cassutto, found the volunteer reviewers by posting a request for participation on several newsgroups and mailing lists. The volunteers, who responded by e-mail, included professors, students, and ordinary people. Their reviews were delivered via e-mail to the students.

PEN PALS

Pen pals on the Internet are called "keypals." (After all, you write with a keyboard, not a pen.) The best keypal friendships grow out of a shared common interest. For instance, you might meet somebody through a newsgroup, or a collaborative Internet project, and begin corresponding via e-mail. If you choose, you might eventually talk on the phone or meet in person. (Show caution before meeting anyone in person. See Chapter Eleven.) But many keypal friendships flourish with simply an exchange of messages.

What about posting a request for a keypal? Such requests are sometimes seen in the k12 newsgroups. Unfortunately, these requests rarely meet with success. In fact, the k12.chat.senior newsgroup specifically discourages posts for keypals. Similarly, classrooms that use mailing lists for teachers to advertise for keypals often receive little or no response.

This is what Carlos A. Rivera, an active newsgroup participant, has to say about posting a keypal request to k12.chat.senior, a newsgroup dedicated to group discussion:

< 109 >

Finding keypals is for soc.penpals and such. We at K12.chat.senior hate penpal requests. All get at least one flame.... Surveys are ok, as long as they are presented in a good way. Discussing issues is the main thing. We discuss anything—politics, abortion, racism, homophobia, music, airheads, history, sports, society, sex—as long as your arguments are valid and you are "mature." (I hate using "mature" at my age (17) ;-) .)

If you simply want to chat with other people your age, check out the k12.chat newsgroups. If you want to practice a foreign language, several k12 newsgroups let you do that, too. But if you want to find a keypal, post a message to newsgroup **soc.penpals** .

Here's what Laura Snider at Crescenta Valley High School in La Crescenta, California, has to say about finding keypals:

I met most—no, all—of my keypals just by posting regular stuff on newsgroups here. I'm really into bad movies, 50s sci-fi and the like, and I posted a couple messages about schlocky films. Something like "Anybody out there who likes really bad movies? Films by Edward D. Wood Jr., Coffin Joe, etc.?" My message was a lot longer than that, but you get my drift. I guess, in a way, it was a request for a keypal, but it ensured that I would have something in common with whoever responded. Four people ended up e-mailing me about bad movies, and I kept in touch with all four of them during the school year.

Making friends on the Internet is really not that different from making friends in person. Be yourself, reveal your interests, show some curiosity toward those you correspond with and, with luck, you'll soon find that you share common

< 110 >

ground with a few people. Many people believe that the Net is a great equalizer, a place where wit, intelligence, and a well-turned phrase matter far more than appearance or social position. For this reason, friendships in cyberspace are truly a meeting of the minds.

< 111 >

PUBLISHING WITH THE WORLD WIDE WEB

The World Wide Web offers a unique opportunity for school groups to publish their work. Without a printing press, or even a copy shop, you can spread your words and artwork around the world. To publish on the Web, at least one person in your group will need to learn how to create Web documents with HyperText Markup Language.

This chapter will provide you with ideas for some of the kinds of Web documents you can create. It will also give you a brief overview of the technical steps you will need to follow.

CREATE A WEB PAGE

Consider creating a World Wide Web page about your school. A Web page is an opportunity for you and your

< 113 >

classmates to tell the cyber community about your-selves, your teachers, and your home town. Here are a few ideas of what you could include in your school's home page:

- Your school crest

- Map showing where in the country your school is located

- Pictures of people in your school

- History of the school

- Description of your community: history, special fea-tures, tourist sites, local businesses and industries

- Class projects, including essays, stories, songs, poems, artwork, and science experiments

- A guest book that invites messages from school alum-ni. (Ask them to leave their e-mail addresses or home page address)

- A news page that gives dates for upcoming events, such as class reunions, retirements, school plays, and fundraisers

- Requests for donations of computers and other equipment your school needs

The best way to get ideas for a school home page is to visit the Web pages of other schools. You can do this by following links from the Web66 site. Hundreds of schools have registered their Web pages with the Web66 home page, maintained by the University of Minnesota College of Education. This Web site is dedicated to providing links to elementary, middle, and high schools on the Internet all over the world.

Web address: **http://web66.coled.umn.edu/schools.html**

< 114 >

NEWSPAPERS AND MAGAZINES ON THE WEB

New online magazines, newspapers, and yearbooks created by students are springing up all over. Here are a few of the publications available on the World Wide Web.

The Vocal Point is an online newspaper directed by students from Centennial Middle School in Boulder, Colorado. Each monthly issue is devoted to a new topic of local or national importance. Past topics include: poverty, the Internet, censorship, and violence.

Each issue includes articles written by students at Centennial Middle School and other schools, as well as links to articles elsewhere on the Internet that are related to their topic. The newspaper is working to include stories written by students who live in other states and countries.

Web address:
http://bvsd.k12.co.us/cent/Newspaper/Newspaper.html

MidLink Magazine is an electronic magazine for students in the middle grades, ages ten to fifteen. The magazine contains art and writing and is meant for middle school kids around the world. Each issue has a theme. MidLink Magazine accepts submissions on computer disks sent through the mail.

Web address:
http://longwood.cs.ucf.edu:80/~MidLink

CyberKids and CyberTeen are two free online magazines published by Mountain Lake Software. The magazine includes articles written by students and by staff members. The first issue of CyberKids contained an article on the first African-American woman in space, an article on ancient Egyptian beliefs, and student artwork.

CyberKids Web address:
http://www.mtlake.com/cyberkids/

< 115 >

CyberTeen Web address:
http://www.mtlake.com/cyberteens/

KIDS + ENCYCLOPEDIA = KIDOPEDIA

A kidopedia is a project that combines sharing observations with publishing on the Internet. Imagine an online encyclopedia with entries written by kids and teens around the world. Each article would be based up on firsthand experience. Under "S," for instance, students at Atlantic View Elementary School in Lawrencetown, Nova Scotia, have contributed an entry to The Best of Kidopedia site about one of their favorite sports: "Winter Surfing." The Website address is: **http://rdz.stjohns.edu/kidopedia/** The kidopedia plans to bring together a diverse range of perspectives and experiences. Some people complain that television is creating one global culture. This kind of endeavor could reverse that trend. The kidopedia promises to be an interesting project.

You and your school can create your own kidopedia and put it on the Internet with a World Wide Web page. Try to fill it with entries that describe activities and things unique to your community. Imagine what people outside your community might like to learn more about. The good thing about a kidopedia is that future classes of students can keep adding to it. Unlike a newspaper, it never grows old.

HOW TO CREATE WEB PAGES

Here are the steps you will need to follow to create your own Web pages. The information here is meant just to get you thinking about the project. You will need to consult an expert resource (like a friend or Web site or a book devoted to Web publishing) to learn all the nitty-gritty details.

1. Decide what Internet service provider is going to

< 116 >

set up your Web pages on its computer. Your Internet access provider may offer you space for your pages at very little cost. Otherwise you will have to shop around for the best deal.

2. Learn HyperText Markup Language (HTML). HTML is a set of codes that tells the Web browser what your text should look like. It is relatively simple to learn. You will also use a word processing program, like the one you use to write school reports. There are many Web sites (and books) that can tell you the specific codes needed to write a HTML document.

3. Decide how to structure your pages. What will be on the home page? What will you name the links to the other pages? Before you begin writing HTML, create a map of your site on a piece of paper.

4. Find interesting URLs (Web addresses) to put in your Web site, if you wish. But remember: too many tantalizing links may detract from your site. Who's going to stay to visit Fox Lane High School's home page if they can jump to the X-Files Web site?
(By the way, the address for the X-Files World Wide Web home page is: **http://glyphs.com/millpop/95/x-files.html**)

5. Graphics: You don't need them but sooner or later you will probably want them. For generic graphics—like a cartoon figure of a football player—you can use clip art from a CD-ROM. For graphics of specific people and places—your school's star quarterback, for instance— you can use a scanner to scan in images of photographs. Black-and-white scanners are much cheaper than color scanners and you can "colorize" the pictures with a computer paint program. There is also a way to download images from the Web itself.

6. Include the e-mail address of your site's Webmaster, the person responsible for maintaining the site. Invite

< 117 >

visitors to e-mail the Webmaster with their comments and suggestions.

7. Advertise your site once it is up and running. Register it with the Web66 site (see page 114). Tell all your keypals. Post polite messages in newsgroups and mailing lists for people who may be interested in the subject matter included at your site.

8. Don't think of your Web site as a project that you finish. That would be like running the same episode of a TV program each week. Changing your Web page and adding to it will keep people coming back for more.

LESSONS IN WEB PUBLISHING: You can turn to the World Wide Web itself for lessons on how to create your own Web pages and use HyperText Markup Language (HTML). Here are some useful sites:

* WWW & HTML Developer's JumpStation

http://oneworld.wa.com/htmldev/devpage/devpage.html

Short tutorial with links to other HTML tutorials and collections of graphics

* A Beginner's Guide to HTML

http://www.ncsa.uiuc.edu/General/Internet/WWW/HTMLPrimer.html

A very complete guide, not for beginners only

* The HTML Sourcebook

http://www.utirc.utoronto.ca/HTMLdocs/NewHTML/intro.html

HTML developer's tutorial

< 118 >

* Introduction to HTML

http://melmac.corp.harris.com/about_html.html

Not a tutorial, but contains links to HTML tutorials and Web graphics

< 119 >

USING THE INTERNET FOR WRITTEN REPORTS

The Internet can take you to vast stores of documents, discussions, and data. In fact, many people mistakenly think of it as exclusively an information source. When you have been assigned a written report or a research project, you may think that the Internet is the first place to turn for information. That's not necessarily true. Although the Internet has much to offer, it should be approached only after careful thought.

Using the Internet will not change the usual steps involved in writing a report. You will still need to choose a topic, find sources of information, research your topic, take notes, develop an outline, write a rough draft, write a final draft, and prepare a bibliography. Those steps are necessary to write a really excellent report.

< 121 >

This chapter will help you make the best use of Internet resources. It will also tell you how to evaluate the sources you find and how to include those sources in your bibliography. But it won't tell you how to write a report. If you need that kind of guidance, you should ask your teacher or librarian to recommend a good book on writing reports.

CHOOSING A RESEARCH TOPIC

Some research projects are better suited for the Internet than others. To decide whether the Internet has the resources that can help you with your project, consider the subjects well-represented on the Net:

Academic disciplines, especially science

Pop culture

Current events and issues

Government documents, statistics, figures, and data

Weather

Images of the moon and Mars taken by NASA

Political candidates

Careers

Hobbies

Books

On the other hand, some topics—especially biography and many episodes of history—are missing from the Net. Also, if you're designing a survey to post, keep in mind that people in cyberspace tend to be better educated than average and to have access to computers. Old people, the very young, and poor people are not well represented on the Net. Men also outnumber women, about 2 to 1.

< 122 >

Ideally, you should consider these strengths and weaknesses before you even choose a research topic. Are you determined to use the Internet for your research? Have you been assigned to use it for a topic? In that case, it makes sense to use the Internet itself to come up with a topic.

Start by browsing. Visit many information sites quickly. Keep track of promising possibilities by using commands in Gopher and the World Wide Web to mark your place.

If you are working on a science project, one of the best places to post a question is the k12.ed.science newsgroup. This newsgroup is populated by students, teachers, and scientists who are quite willing to assist anyone seeking information. Students often use the newsgroup to gather information for research projects. Recent projects have included studies of how people live near volcanoes or earthquake zones, climatology projects, and information on how to design a spaceship engineered to fly to Mars or Venus, says Michael Ochs, professor of physics at Haverford College and moderator of k12.ed.science.

HOW TO SHOP FOR A RESEARCH TOPIC

✓ Browse Gopherspace. Select menu choices that look interesting.

✓ Lurk in a few newsgroups. To find newsgroups relevant to your topic, use Deja News, a Web site that will conduct a keyword search among recent archived newsgroups. If you wished to write a report on teen pregnancy, for example, you would type "teen pregnancy" as your keywords and Deja News would return with a list of newsgroup messages in which that subject had been discussed.

Web address: **http://www.dejanews.com/**

< 123 >

Ninth-grader Silas Hoxie of Evanston Township High
School in Evanston, Illinois, used both the Internet and
traditional library resources to focus his space science
project. Silas knew he wanted to research some aspect of
supernovas. After posting a message to the sci.astronomy
newsgroup, he received e-mail from a professor of astro-
physics who provided him with the addresses of several
relevant Web sites. After examining those Web sites, Silas
chose to focus on neutrino emissions.

Once you have come up with several possible topics,
adopt a more careful approach. At this stage, you're finished with browsing. Now you want to determine how
much material related to your topic is available. You
need to do an organized search. This search will help you
determine whether your topic is too broad (too much
material) or too narrow (not enough), as discussed in
Chapter Five.

How to Focus Your Topic

✓ Do a keyword search in Gopherspace. (In other
words, use Veronica.)

✓ Use World Wide Web directories to do a subject
search. Visit those Web sites. Go ahead and follow
links as long as they are relevant to your topic.
Look for descriptions of relevant gophers and
newsgroups.

✓ Post a polite message in a relevant newsgroup
asking for help with your topic. Ask people to sug-
gest useful resources, including the addresses
(URLs) of relevant Gophers and WWW sites.

< 124 >

If you can't seem to find any resources related to your topic, don't give up. Try choosing other keywords to describe your topic. Perhaps it's indexed under a synonym you haven't thought of. Or maybe you need to broaden your topic somewhat. Consider, too, that while the Internet may have little related to your topic, traditional sources, like books, may contain lots. It might just be that your topic falls into one of the weak areas of the Net. (Of course, this still isn't good news if you're determined to use the Net to research your topic.)

Kerene Tayloe of Evanston Township High School in Evanston, Illinois, spent several weeks with a telescope looking for sunspots without success. Frustrated, she turned to the Web for help. There she found a site that listed charts of recent sunspot activity—and discovered that there had been no activity on the days she had looked. She sent e-mail to the experts whose addresses were listed in the Web site and received replies that pointed her toward other useful Web sites.

Probably the best way to guarantee that the Net will have the material you need for your topic is to develop a project about the Internet itself. For example, you could write about online publications for kids and teenagers.

Even if you discover that the Internet has your topic well covered, don't neglect the usual sources. The Internet cannot replace a library! Only a very, very few current books are available through the Net. Not many magazines are available either. For most topics, you will still need to visit the library.

Your library may have magazines and newspapers available through a computerized system called Infotrac. This is different from the Internet.

< 125 >

TOPIC FIRST, INTERNET RESEARCH SECOND

In many instances, you'll have your research topic first, before you can browse the Internet. Perhaps a topic was assigned to you. Or perhaps you have a strong desire to write about a particular subject, regardless of whether you can research it with the Internet or not. In this case, the features of the Internet will merely be among the many resources you use.

When you begin researching your subject, figure out how the Internet fits into your research strategy. Quickly do an organized search of the Net to see how well it covers your subject. You may find the Internet very useful, somewhat useful, or not at all useful.

Spend a few minutes jotting down the books, articles, and Internet features you plan to examine for information. Decide which ones you will browse through first. This list will make up your research strategy. A research strategy will help you work effectively. Your strategy need not be long or complicated. Keep it flexible but focused. With a strategy in hand, you will be less easily distracted by the interesting, yet irrelevant, items you are bound to run across. This is especially true on the World Wide Web when a single point-and-click can launch you far off course!

In general, use the Internet for ideas and information you can't find elsewhere. Don't search the Net looking for information you could easily find in a general reference book, like an encyclopedia or atlas. Subjects that have entire books written about them—such as the Persian Gulf War, for instance—are not likely to be covered any more thoroughly on the Net.

On the other hand, the Internet is a great place to find discussions of current events. If you have a contemporary topic, and are spending most of your time reading current magazines and newspapers, it's a good bet that the Internet also has relevant, up-to-the-minute information, especially in the newsgroups. Similarly, topics relat-

< 126 >

ed to popular culture, especially television, film, and music, are also easily found on the Internet, especially the Web.

The Net may also be the right place to turn for new developments on an old topic. If you're researching the Persian Gulf War, for example, you may wish to use the Net to follow the discussion regarding the claim that the Gulf War left many veterans suffering from unusual illnesses. Conducting a keyword search of "Gulf War syndrome" in Deja News, for instance, turned up discussions in five newsgroups: alt.desert-storm.facts, sci.environment, sci.military.naval, misc.health.alternative, and talk.environment.

For a research project on disease control, Tong Chieng of Westview Centennial Secondary School in North York, Ontario, started with Gopher to find statistics and other data. Then he posted to a newsgroup concerned with disease and received four responses in twenty-four hours. "Of course, not all of the information received is always useful," says Tong, "but that's part of the fun. One of the responses told me where to look for these stats, and one had two pages of literature on the World Health Organization, and the rest was useless stuff. I then went a little off topic and started surfing elsewhere on the Web."

Finally, let the Internet send you back to the library. If a newsgroup is chatting about a particular newspaper article, go read the article yourself. Perhaps the newsgroup is condemning a particular current event or government announcement. Find out as much as you can about the event or announcement from other sources. What are news magazines, newspapers, and other news-

< 127 >

groups saying about it? Only by looking at other sources can you discover the full spectrum of opinion regarding an event. This will help you better understand both the event and the newsgroup's reaction. If you hear a book or newsletter or magazine mentioned on the Net, follow that lead and look at the material yourself.

INTERVIEWING ONLINE

With the Internet, you can very easily interview for information. Are you interested in people's thoughts and opinions? Reactions to a current event? Consider posting your questions in the appropriate newsgroup or mailing list. If you have a question related to science, post it to the k12.ed.science newsgroup. The Global SchoolNet has a Scientist-on-Tap from the Jet Propulsion Laboratory who will answer questions posted by students. Visit the Web site **http://www.gsn.org/gsn/articles/article.sot.html** . You can also locate a scientist through the Mad Scientist Network at **http://medinfo.wustl.edu/~yst/msn/** .

Be as courteous as possible when you interview on the Internet. Before posting your request, spend some time lurking in the relevant newsgroup or mailing list to get a feel for the people there. Read the newsgroup's FAQ. Keep your questions specific. Above all, don't treat a newsgroup like an encyclopedia or, even worse, like a faceless computer resource. No one is willing to do your work for you. If you have questions that could easily be answered with a trip to the library, make the trip to the library. If your questions show that you are being lazy, you will annoy people and you will risk getting flamed.

When you're ready to post your questions, be very clear about who you are, what you're doing, and why. State whether you would prefer people to send you e-mail directly or post their replies to the newsgroup.

< 128 >

(Unless you're sure the subject is of interest to the news-group's members, ask for replies by e-mail.)

Here's what *not* to do:

> *My name is Liz Marshall and I'm writing a report about gene therapy. Please send me e-mail about everything you know about gene therapy. My paper is due tomorrow. I am in the 11th grade at Fox Lane High School in Bedford, New York. I am eager to hear from you.*

Here's a much better request:

> *My name is Liz Marshall and I'm writing a report about gene therapy. I read a newspaper report that said scientists think that gene therapy was working for a cystic fibrosis patient but they couldn't say for absolute sure. I don't understand why the scientists couldn't say for sure whether it was or was not working. Can you help me? My paper is due in one week. I am in the 11th grade at Fox Lane High School in Bedford, New York. I am eager to hear from you.*

See the difference?

Don't be disappointed if you receive responses that are very short. It may take two or three exchanges of e-mail before you get replies with the amount of detail that you need. People may be unwilling to devote a lot of energy to a response until they know you are actually going to read it. The best thing to do after you get your first set of responses is to respond to them immediately. First, thank people for responding. Then politely press them for more information. You may need to encourage them to answer very specifically by asking very specific questions. (Some people may answer at length in response to broad, open-ended questions, but that strategy works much better in face-to-face interviews than over the Internet.)

< 129 >

When sophomore Jerry Fors was invited by his English teacher, Chris K. Davis, to use the Internet to research a topic of his choice, he chose politics for his project. He posted questions to alt.politics, alt. republican, and other groups. He also used Veronica to search through Gopher for political party platforms.

Other topics chosen by students in Davis's class at Crescenta Valley High School, La Crescenta, California, included: What is it like to play college softball? What do attorneys do? Should I believe in God? In addition to traditional library sources, the students used newsgroups to gain an added perspective on their topic.

With some subjects, you might be able to gather the information you need just by entering into the conversation of a newsgroup. Rather than arrive armed with your own agenda, you could just pose questions relevant to the subject being discussed.

EVALUATING INFORMATION FOUND ON THE INTERNET

Using the Internet doesn't change most of the steps involved in writing a research paper. The Net does pose unique problems, however, when it comes to evaluating the information you find. Evaluating information means examining facts carefully to determine whether they are accurate. It means determining how a source is biased. If experts disagree about a particular matter, it means working hard to understand why they disagree.

Evaluating information can be difficult even with traditional library resources, like newspapers and magazines. With some features of the Internet, evaluation can be nearly impossible. That doesn't mean you don't both-

< 130 >

er to do it—quite the contrary! Instead, you need to pay careful attention to which facts can be verified and which ones cannot.

Facts found in Gopherspace and the World Wide Web are usually easier to evaluate than information exchanged in newsgroups or mailing lists. Here are a few general guidelines for using Gopherspace and the World Wide Web for written reports:

First, determine where your facts are coming from. THIS IS A MUST! You can't begin to verify and attribute facts without this step. Is the information coming from a familiar institution, like a university, government agency, commercial company, nonprofit organization, or museum? Knowing the institution makes evaluating the information easier.

Take note of possible bias once you've identified where the facts are coming from. Is this information being promoted by a company that is also trying to sell its products? Does the organization have a political agenda? Is the government giving you all sides of a controversial issue?

Do you know the source? If the information comes from some place you've never heard of, find out more about it. Have your teacher or parents or friends heard of this place? How does the institution describe itself? How is it described by reporters or other commentators? How is it viewed by other segments of society? If you discover controversy concerning the group, do your best to understand what the controversy is and why it matters.

Don't hesitate to verify. If you find discrepancies, or information that sounds unlikely, try to understand the reason for inconsistencies and contradictions. Also, if experts disagree, try to find out why.

< 131 >

Describe your sources. If you find information that you can't verify, be sure that your report clearly states where the information came from. Give the Gopher or Web address of your source and a short description of the agency that served the information. If the information is disputed, state that, too, and briefly explain the controversy.

Information discovered in newsgroups and mailing lists poses special challenges. Facts found here can be very valuable, but also very difficult to verify. Approach these groups with an extra dose of common sense and skepticism. Put facts found here to this three-point test:

1. Is the information you wish to use in your report a fact that needs to be verified? Or is it an opinion?

2. How has the person expressing the idea represented himself or herself? Is he or she speaking as an employee of an organization or as a private individual? You may never learn the real name of the person writing the message. It can be very difficult—sometimes impossible—to determine the credentials of the person expressing an opinion.

3. Can you verify the information? Can your source help you do this? Information that you can't verify or attribute to a source should not be used.

CITING INFORMATION FOUND ON THE INTERNET

When you write a report, you need to include where you found your information. You can do this within the report, with footnotes, or in a bibliography. Your teacher will tell you the best format to follow.

Many guides exist to tell you how to cite information found in traditional library sources. The proper way to cite Internet information is still evolving, however. In

< 132 >

general, you will need to describe the title of the information, the author, the date, and its address (URL). For e-mail and newsgroups, you will give the writer's name, the date, the subject of the message, and the writer's e-mail address. A recent book on this issue is *Electronic Style: A Guide to Citing Electronic Information* by Xia Li and Nancy B. Crane (Meckler Publishing, Westport, CT, 1993). This book provides a standard format for citing everything from Gophers to newsgroup messages with multiple topics.

You won't always be able to provide the full names of the people who write messages in cyberspace, however. In many cases, e-mail addresses include only initials or screen nicknames. If possible, send e-mail asking for the person's real name. If you must cite your source with just the nickname, add a note telling your teacher and other readers that the screen name is not necessarily the person's real name.

Reporters are treating messages that appear on the Internet as public speech and including them in news stories. But confirming the identity of people in cyberspace is a big challenge. Some journalists believe that even knowing a person's real name from an e-mail message is not enough. To ensure accuracy, reporters are also telephoning online informants and asking if they are the actual authors of the messages that bear their name. Others think phone calls aren't necessary. It's an ongoing debate.

< 133 >

ELEVEN

PLAYING IT SAFE ON THE INTERNET

It is enormously exciting to be part of a community as large and as diverse as the Internet. Yet this cyberspace community is like any other big city. Most of its citizens are basically honest and well-meaning. Others are deceitful and sly and best approached with caution. A tiny fraction of the population is downright dangerous. With common sense, however, you can easily keep yourself safe.

The Internet is a great place to test your ideas and express your opinions. Feel free to engage in vigorous debate with others. But when it comes to revealing personal information about yourself—particularly your address and phone number—you should be extremely careful. You must also show caution when you decide to meet a keypal face-to-face.

< 135 >

The reason for this is that people on the Internet may not be who they claim to be. At times, after all, you may choose not to reveal your young age so that other people online take you more seriously. In the same manner, adults may pose as teenagers to gain the trust of kids and teens. Men may pose as women or girls. Granted, you can be almost certain that someone who says she is a fifteen-year-old girl is exactly that, but it is worth reserving a tiny bit of doubt, especially when you make plans to get together in person. Don't forget that e-mail addresses can also be disguised.

EDUCATE YOUR PARENTS

Your parents may be worried about your safety on the Internet. They may have heard lurid stories about adults exploiting children and teens they met online. They might worry about your exposure to sexual or violent images on the Net. If your parents barely understand what the Internet is, they might feel helpless in the face of these presumed dangers.

The best way to reassure your parents is to educate them. Get them involved. Give them this book to read. If your school has an open house that features its use of the Internet, make sure your parents attend. Sit down together at the computer terminal and impress them with educational Web or Gopher sites. Let them read e-mail from teachers and scientists. Tell them about Internet projects that your school is participating in. Describe the Web pages or Gopher that your school is designing. Emphasize that the Internet is a dynamic, ever-changing place filled with people from all over the world. Visiting it is a lot like attending college or taking a trip to a big city: it involves some risks, but very, very many rewards.

You may want to remind them that the Internet is not like television. You are in charge of the material that appears on the computer screen. Scenes with violent or sexual content don't just appear randomly. In fact, it

< 136 >

takes a certain amount of computer expertise to download and display files containing pictures.

The best way to calm your parents is to assure them that the moral values you hold in other areas of your life will extend to your participation in the Internet community. In other words, if they trust you not to look at dirty magazines at your friends' houses, and to show caution when a stranger approaches you at the mall, they should also be able to trust you to act responsibly on the Internet. Perhaps you can agree upon a set of rules for Internet use at home and at school. Here is a sample of the kind of agreement you might wish to use with your parents:

My Rules for Online Safety

I will not give out personal information such as my address, telephone number, parents' work address/telephone number, or the name and location of my school without my parents' permission.

I will tell my parents right away if I come across any information that makes me feel uncomfortable.

I will never agree to get together with someone I "meet" online without first checking with my parents. If my parents agree to the meeting, I will be sure that it is in a public place and bring my mother or father along.

I will never send a person my picture or anything else without first checking with my parents.

I will not respond to any messages that are mean or in any way make me feel uncomfortable. It is not my fault if I get a message like that. If I do, I will tell my parents right away so that they can contact the online service.

I will talk with my parents so that we can set up rules for going online. We will decide upon the time of day that I can be online, the length of time I can be online, and appropriate areas for me to visit. I will not access other areas or break these rules without their permission.

< 137 >

Your school may also ask you to sign a similar agreement that outlines acceptable use of the Internet while at school.

"My Rules for Online Safety" is from a booklet titled *Child Safety on the Information Highway*. The brochure was jointly produced by the National Center for Missing and Exploited Children and the Interactive Services Association, and was written by Lawrence J. Magid. It is sponsored by America Online, CompuServe, Delphi Internet, e-world, GEnie, Interchange Online Network, and Prodigy Service. The full text is available on major online services, or call the center at 800-843-5678.

You can see another sample acceptable-use agreement by visiting the World Wide Web home page of the Los Alamos Middle School in Los Alamos, New Mexico:
http://lams.losalamos.k12.nm.us/accept.html

ANGRY AND OBSCENE MESSAGES

Unfortunately, some people who are perfectly polite in person become very aggressive in their e-mail messages. They write angry notes and insult anyone who disagrees with their thoughts. Don't become this type of person. Make it a habit never to reply immediately to an e-mail message that angers or upsets you. Give yourself time to cool off and then reread the message. Is it possible that you've misunderstood something? Could the message be sarcastic?

Always remember that real people with real feelings are receiving your e-mail messages. Don't use foul language or send obscene messages. If you see another student causing trouble by sending cruel messages, ask why he or she is doing this. Tell the person that the Internet

< 138 >

needs him or her to contribute in a constructive, positive manner. Perhaps such a student would enjoy building Web pages or leading a collaborative project.

What if you receive a nasty message from a stranger? Don't respond. Show the message to your teacher and parents. Contact your Internet service provider. Most important of all, don't take it personally. This person doesn't know you. Think about how you would feel if you were walking past an unfamiliar gang of teens and they made rude comments to you. Sure, it hurts, but it's their problem, not yours.

For a fascinating account of catching an Internet obscene caller, read "Ballad of an E-mail Terrorist." The article describes tracking down an obscene message sender. When the culprit, a high school student, is finally caught and confronted, he explains that he received rude messages while on the Internet and thought that sending obscene messages was an acceptable game. He failed to think about what he was doing and whose feelings he might hurt. The story is part of the Global SchoolNet Foundation Web site.

Web address:
http://www.gsn.org/gsn/articles/article.email.ballad.html

SIFTING THROUGH FACT AND FICTION

If you saw a magazine ad for a sure-fire way to make money fast, what would you think? If someone told you about a tonic that instantly cured the common cold, would you believe it? What if you saw a television interview with a woman who declared that the Holocaust never happened? Would you accept her claim?

Never assume that just because information appears on the Internet that it has been verified. The Internet is full of false health claims and get-rich-quick schemes. Show caution when reading such claims. Before accept-

< 139 >

ing any unfamiliar ideas as true, consider their source and investigate them thoroughly.

You may also find that the Internet contains people who think very differently than you do about a wide range of subjects. At times, you may feel that your own beliefs are being threatened. Especially disturbing are those newsgroups filled with expressions of hate and violence. It is dangerous to ignore such opinions, as history shows again and again. But if reading messages in certain newsgroups causes you a great deal of anguish, don't do it. And talk over what you're reading with a trusted adult.

PORNOGRAPHY ON THE INTERNET

If you are ever sent pornographic material, either through e-mail or on files, notify your teacher, parents, and computer system administrator at once. While surfing the Internet, you may inadvertently stumble across obscene material or images. Such material is currently legal; to avoid it merely avoid those sites. Child pornography, however, is illegal. If you see child pornography on the Net, notify your teacher and parents and immediately report it to the National Center for Missing and Exploited Children (800-843-5678).

The U.S. Congress passed a bill that outlawed the transmission of sexually explicit material on the Internet. The law, known as the Communications Decency Act of 1996, imposes fines up to $100,000 and two-year prison terms on anyone who knowingly transmits "obscene, lewd, lascivious, filthy or indecent" communications on the Internet. The Communications Decency Act was a small part of a large bill, the Telecommunications Act of 1996.

Computer users and civil-liberties groups challenged the law in court. They argued that the law prevents free speech, a right protected by the Constitution. They also

< 140 >

observed that the law would be impossible to enforce. On the World Wide Web, many sites showed their support for free speech by adding an image of a blue ribbon to their pages.

Despite the ultimate fate of the Communications Decency Act, it prompted general agreement that it was reasonable for schools and parents to try and limit children's access to online pornography and hate speech. Here are some of the ways that might be done:

Ratings system. Ratings, similar to those used by the motion picture industry, would be assigned to World Wide Web sites. A group known as the Platform for Internet Content Selection, made up of over fifty-five computer companies, began working on a ratings system in 1995. As planned, the rating of a given site could be determined before actually visiting the site.

Limiting access to only a few newsgroups. Certain newsgroups are full of sexual material or hate speech. By limiting access to only a few select newsgroups, schools prevent student access to the controversial newsgroups. Of course, subscribing to just the k12 newsgroups is only a limited solution, since objectionable material often comes from kids and teens themselves.

Blocking software. These computer programs are programmed to automatically block out specific material. A software program called SurfWatch is intended to block out sexually explicit material anywhere on the Net, including the Web, Gopher sites, and newsgroups. If a computer user tries to access one of the forbidden sites, SurfWatch displays a colorful logo reading "Blocked by SurfWatch" instead. There are drawbacks to this approach, however. Blocking software cannot keep up with the new sites that appear daily. In addition, any one of the sites on the list of forbidden sites could simply change its name to avoid detection.

< 141 >

Yes, there is obscene material on the Internet. There is also obscene material in the corner grocery store. Life in cyberspace is an extension of real life: although many good, decent people can be found here, it has its share of idiots and creeps, too. If you approach your exploration of the Internet with enthusiasm and good faith, you are certain to meet others in cyberspace who share your desire to communicate and learn. At the very least, the Internet is a printing press, a tool for private and mass communication, and a storehouse of information. And at most? It's still so new that some people believe its potential has yet to be fully realized. Enjoy the trip.

< 142 >

Internet Resources

HOW TO FIND COLLABORATIVE PROJECTS ON THE INTERNET

These sites are all good places to start looking for collaborative projects. Many of the World Wide Web sites are linked to each other and to the Gopher sites as well.

World Wide Web Sites for Collaborative Projects

▶ WWW servers for Education hosted at CNIDR (The Center for Networked Information Discovery and Retrieval):

http://k12.cnidr.org/

One of the best places to start your search, this also contains links to the next three sites.

▶ EdWeb

http://k12.cnidr.org:90/

Includes the "EdWeb k-12 Resource Guide."

▶ Janice's K12 Cyberspace Outpost

http://k12.cnidr.org/janice_k12/k12menu.html

This site is frequently updated.

< 143 >

ArtsEdge

http://artsedge.kennedy-center.org/artsedge.html

For arts education projects.

 Global SchoolNet Foundation

http://www.gsn.org

From the home page, click on "Global Schoolhouse." Then click on "Internet Projects Registry and Matrix." Or go straight to:

http://www.gsn.org/gsn/proj/index.html

The Global SchoolNet Foundation is committed to providing a central location and registry for Internet projects. It maintains a monthly calendar of current projects.

 InforMNs

http://informns.k12.mn.us

InforMNs (Internet for Minnesota Schools) was the sponsor of Journey North and Mayaquest. Among its projects are those designed for schools with e-mail access only. (InforMNs also has a Gopher.)

 NASA Education Sites—Quest!

http://quest.arc.nasa.gov

Select "Online Interactive Projects."

http://quest.arc.nasa.gov/interactive.html

 Dewey Web

http://ics.soe.umich.edu

The University of Michigan clearinghouse of information and projects service.

KIDLINK

http://www.kidlink.org/

The KIDLINK Society is dedicated to encouraging dialogue among ten-to fifteen-year-olds around the world. Its headquar-

< 144 >

ters is in Norway. (The KIDLINK Society also has a Gopher and sponsors several mailing lists.)

▶ Earth Day Grocery Bag Project
http://www.halcyon.com/arborhts/faq.html
This is the project described in Chapter Eight.

Mailing Lists for Collaborative Projects

The Global SchoolNet Foundation sponsors a moderated list of classroom projects called HILITES. The list is available to K-12 teachers and their supervised students.

Send an e-mail message to: **majordomo@gsn.org**
Leave the subject line blank.
In the body of the message type: subscribe hilites

The KIDLINK Society maintains KIDFORUM, a list for dialogue and exchange on a series of specified topics. To subscribe to the list, send an e-mail message to: **listserv@vm1.nodak.edu**

In the body of the message type:
sub KIDFORUM <your name>

Gophers for Collaborative Projects

▶ The Common Knowledge: Pittsburgh Gopher
gopher://gopher.pps.pgh.pa.us
First select "K12 Internet Resources." Then select "Internet Classroom Projects."

▶ InforMNs
InforMNs was the sponsor of Journey North and Mayaquest. Among its projects are those designed for schools with e-mail access only.
gopher://informns.k12.mn.us

< 145 >

Select "Best of the K12 Internet Resources" for a list of collaborative projects.

OTPAD
New York Gopher service
> **gopher://unix5.nysed.gov**
Select "Projects for Collaboration."

 KIDLINK
> **gopher://global.kidlink.org**
Select "KIDLINK in the Classroom." Then select "KIDPROJ Activities." Or go straight to:
> **gopher://global.kidlink.org:70/11/classrooms/kidproj/**

FINDING MORE FUN
Gophers for Fun
Gopherspace is very easy to move through, following your own path of discovery. Here are a few addresses to get you started.

 University of Michigan Library Gopher
> **gopher://gopher.lib.umich.edu**
You can get everywhere from here.

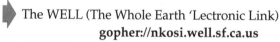 The WELL (The Whole Earth 'Lectronic Link)
> **gopher://nkosi.well.sf.ca.us**
The WELL's menu items include 'zines, cyberpunk, environmental issues, and even the Grateful Dead. The WELL is based in San Francisco.

 Professional Sports Schedules
> **gopher://gopher.bsu.edu/**

 Historical Documents
> **gopher://vax.queens.lib.ny.us**

< 146 >

Select "Social Sciences/History." Then select "Historical documents."

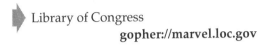
Library of Congress
gopher://marvel.loc.gov

Mailing Lists for Fun

Although it's possible to obtain a long list of available mailing lists, that's not a very effective way to find a mailing list of interest. If you have a special interest, search through magazines, newspapers, newsgroups and World Wide Web pages related to your interest for a mention of relevant mailing lists. You can also use the World Wide Web itself to find mailing lists on specific topics.

Go to TILE.NET located at: **http://tile.net/**
There you can search for relevant mailing lists (and newsgroups) by using keywords.

The KIDLINK Society maintains Global Youth Dialog, eight mailing lists. To receive information on Global Youth Dialog, send an e-mail message to **listserv@vm1.nodak.edu** .
In the body of the message type: **GET KIDCAFE GUIDE**

These are the eight Global Youth Dialog lists:

KIDCAFE—INDIVIDUAL	Individual keypals
KIDCAFE—SCHOOL	School-organized keypals
KIDCAFE—TOPICS	Open discussion
KIDCAFE—QUERY	For students posting questions and polls
KIDCAFE—SPANISH	Keypals writing in Spanish
KIDCAFE—JAPANESE	
KIDCAFE—NORDIC	
KIDCAFE—PORTUGUESE	

< 147 >

To subscribe to one of these lists, send an e-mail message to the address above.

In the body of the message type:
sub <list name> <your name>

The EdWeb K-12 Resource Guide gives the addresses of many mailing lists that are of interest to kids and teens.

Go to EdWeb **http://k12.cnidr.org:90/**

Select "Online Discussion Groups and Electronic Journals" or go directly to http://k12.cnidr.org:90/lists.html

 CHILDRENS-VOICE
Publishes the writing of students ages five to fourteen
listproc@schoolnet.carleton.ca

▶ KIDINTRO
Keypal group for children
listserv@sjuvm.stjohns.edu

▶ MY-VIEW
Global creative writing exchange
listserv@sjuvm.stjohns.edu

▶ PENPAL-L
Keypal exchange
listserv@unccvm.uncc.edu

▶ TALKBACK
News exchange and discussion for students
listserv@sjuvm.stjohns.edu

The following are two mailing lists that spotlight Internet resources. Subscribing to these lists is an easy way to become more familiar with what the Internet has to offer:

< 148 >

The Internet TourBus
listserv@listserv.aol.com

Scout Report
listserv@lists.internic.net

World Wide Web Sites for Fun

Use the Web directories listed on pages 98 and 99 to help you find Web sites of interest. Here are a few sites to get you started:

NASA Space Shuttle Home Page
http://shuttle.nasa.gov/

Dinosaur Hall
http://ucmp1.berkeley.edu/exhibittext/dinosaur.html

Comics
http://www.uta.fi/yhteydet/personalhl.html

Center for Mars Exploration
http://cmex-www.arc.nasa.gov/

Electronic Newsstand
http://www.enews.com

The White House
http://www.whitehouse.gov/WH/welcome.html

Green Eggs
http://ibd.ar.com/ger/

< 149 >

Want to find more Web sites? Want to see what WWW sites have been discussed in your favorite newsgroup? Green Eggs is a WWW site that indexes the URLs mentioned in newsgroups.

GUIDES TO THE INTERNET

Does your computer system use commands that weren't discussed in this book? Try one of these guides for a more comprehensive look at the Internet.

Gibbs, Mark. *Navigating the Internet*. Indianapolis: Howard W. Sams & Co., 1994.

Glister, Paul. *Finding it on the Internet: The Essential Guide to Archie, Veronica, Gopher, WAIS, WWW and Other Search Tools*. New York: John Wiley & Sons, 1994.

Kent, Peter. *The Complete Idiot's Guide to the Internet*. Topanga, CA: Alpha Books, 1994.

Kent, Peter. *The Complete Idiot's Guide to the World Wide Web*. Topanga, CA: Alpha Books, 1995.

Levine, John R. *Internet for Dummies*. Foster City, CA: IDS Books, 1993

< 150 >

Glossary

Alias: a short word used in place of a long e-mail address.

Anonymous ftp: by entering the login name "anonymous" at many ftp sites, you can gain access to the file archives there and move copies of the files to your own computer.

Archie: search tool that looks through computer file archives for the location of a particular file.

Archives: storage area for computer files.

Article: a message that appears in a newsgroup.

BBS (See Bulletin Board System)

Blocking software: computer programs designed to block access to known Internet sites containing pornography.

Bookmark: a feature in Gopher and the World Wide Web that you can use to mark Internet sites you have visited in order to return to them quickly and easily.

Bulletin Board System: a network that depends upon telephone dial-up access with a modem. BBSs operate like miniature versions of commercial online services but they usually focus on a single hobby or interest.

Card catalog (See History list)

Case-sensitive: lowercase and uppercase letters are not interchangeable. Changing the form of the letters will change the command.

CD-ROM: compact disc with graphics and sound.

< 151 >

Clip art: graphics without copyright protection that are available to one and all for any purpose.

Commercial online service: a for-profit enterprise that uses the telephone system to create a community of connected subscribers. CompuServe, Prodigy, Delphi Internet, GEnie, and Microsoft Network are examples of commercial online services.

Cross-posting: sending the same message to two or more newsgroups.

Cyberspace: the place created by millions of people communicating via the Internet. Debate and discussion takes place in cyberspace.

Document trail (See History list)

Domain: the information in an electronic mail address that routes the message to a particular institution or office.

Electronic town square: nickname for the Internet that emphasizes how it can be used to encourage debate and discussion.

Emoticon: a symbol designed to make the emotional tone of Internet correspondence very clear. Read sideways, emoticons look like sad or smiley faces.

FAQ: abbreviation for Frequently Asked Questions. Prepared statements in response to frequently asked questions on the Internet. Many newsgroups have FAQs (pronounced "facts").

File transfer protocol (ftp): a feature used to move files between computers. Many computer archives permit you to move copies of files from their site to your own computer. (See also Anonymous ftp)

Flame: an insult or other angry response to a newsgroup article. When flames are exchanged, it is known as a "flame war."

Frequently Asked Questions (See FAQ)

Free-Net: a community-based network that links local electronic resources, from the library card catalog to calendars of community events to government information.

< 152 >

FTP (See File transfer protocol)

Gopher: a feature that offers you a menu of choices to help you select the information you want. Menu selections very often lead to more menus and more choices.

Gopher client: a program on a computer that allows you to access Gopher.

Gopher server: information made available on the Gopher system by an organization. Universities, the government, and museums are among those with Gopher servers.

Gopherspace: the entire Gopher system.

History list: a list of sites visited during a session on the World Wide Web; also known as a "card catalog" or "document trail," depending upon your Web browser.

Home page: the first page that appears when you go to a Web document. The first page that appears when you start your web browser is *your* home page.

Hotlist: a list of bookmarks for the World Wide Web. (See Bookmark)

HTML (HyperText Markup Language): the simple code used to write Web pages.

Hypertext: a document on the Web that contains links allowing you to jump from one part of the document to another. Links can be icons or highlighted words. They allow you to create your own path through a document.

Information superhighway: nickname for the Internet that emphasizes how it can be used to circulate information.

Internet: a worldwide communications system that allows millions of computers to exchange information such as computer files, written messages, graphics, and even sound and video. The Internet is often described as a "network of networks" because it links together over 6,000 smaller computer networks.

Internet Relay Chat: a feature that allows you to carry on a written dialogue with other people who are connected to the Internet at the same time you are.

< 153 >

Internet service provider: local company that provides Internet access for a monthly fee.

IRC (See Internet Relay Chat)

Keypal: Internet penpal.

Keyword: search word.

Kidopedia: online encyclopedia with entries written by kids.

Link: device that connects two Web documents. Links are typically icons or highlighted words that permit you to jump from one document to another with just a click of your computer mouse or a keyword command.

Listserv (See Mailing lists)

Login name: the name used to gain access to a computer account.

Lurking: reading newsgroup articles without posting articles of your own.

Mail program: a program on a computer that allows you to read and send written messages known as electronic mail.

Mailer (See Mail program)

Mailing lists: discussion group that is distributed using electronic mail.

Menu: a directory of choices.

Modem: a device that connects a personal computer to the telephone system.

Moderated newsgroup: a newsgroup whose content is controlled by a person. Articles sent to a moderated newsgroup are evaluated for content and length.

Net: nickname for the Internet.

Netiquette: code of manners that governs behavior on the Internet.

Network: a group of two or more computers connected to exchange files, messages, and other information.

Network news: another name for newsgroups.

Newbie: insulting term for an Internet newcomer who reveals his or her inexperience.

< 154 >

Newsgroup: discussion group where people exchange ideas, share information, provide support, and sometimes argue.

News reader: a program on a computer that allows you to read and send newsgroup articles.

Post: to send an article to a newsgroup.

Scanner: device used to transform photographs or other images into graphics on the World Wide Web.

Screen name: the nickname selected by a subscriber to commercial online services to use in place of his or her real name; often refers to a hobby or special interest.

Smiley face (See Emoticon)

Subscribe: 1. to request that a particular newsgroup appears in your newsreader. 2. to send an e-mail message asking to be added to a mailing list.

Telnet: a feature used to make a connection to a remote computer.

Thread: a series of articles in a newsgroup all related to the same subject.

Uniform Resource Locator (URL): the address of a resource on the Internet.

UNIX: the computer operating system used by most computers with a direct connection to the Internet.

USENET: the system that distributes newsgroups.

Veronica: search tool that takes a specific keyword and looks through the menus in Gopherspace for that keyword. The result is a menu that lists resources with the keyword in their menu titles.

Web: nickname for the World Wide Web.

Web browser: program used to access the World Wide Web. Netscape, Lynx, and Mosaic are examples of Web browsers.

World Wide Web: a feature that links together thousands of different information sources. These information sources contain text and pictures, and sometimes sound and video.

< 155 >

Index

< 157 >

< 158 >

< 159 >